THINK BIGGER

Image © 2020 Dan Steiner

THINK

BIGGER

How I Grew My Accounting Business
to a Point I was Able to Sell One Division for Over
ONE MILLION DOLLARS!

Dan Steiner

With a Foreword by Barbara Weltman

Steiner
BOOKS

For information about special discounts for bulk purchases or author
interviews, appearances, and speaking engagements please contact:

> Steiner Business Solutions
> 2727 Enterprise Parkway
> Suite 105
> Henrico, VA 23294
> dsteiner@steinerbusinesssolutions.com
> (866) 314-6632

First Edition

Edited, cover, and interior design by Rodney Miles:
www.rodneymiles.com

"You were designed for accomplishment, engineered for success, and endowed with the seeds of greatness."

—Zig Ziglar

CONTENTS

Foreword By Barbara Weltman.. ix

Preface... xiii

[1] Identify Your Goals 1

[2] How Do I Get IDEAL Clients? 7

[3] Marketing, Messaging, Branding 21

[4] Pricing & Contracts... 41

[5] Risk – Be Honest!... 70

[6] When and How to Hire... 84

[7] Identifying New Revenue Streams............................ 105

[8] Growth Strategy ~ Organic versus Acquisition 119

[9] Maximize the Value of Your Business 134

[10] Exit Strategy 151

Appendix A: Indispensable Marketing............................. 162

About the Author... 166

Learn More 168

Please Leave a Review... 169

FOREWORD

BY BARBARA WELTMAN

BELIEVE IT OR NOT, government statistics show that about 2,800 businesses start up in the U.S. every day. But of these businesses, many will fail and only a limited number will grow bigger. So here's the point: There's no shortage of entrepreneurial spirit to get started, but there isn't enough knowledge to take a company to the next level. Here's where *Think Bigger* comes in.

I know about the need for the guidance that *Think Bigger* provides on how to scale up because I've seen and dealt with many companies over the years that have struggled to survive and didn't have a clue about how to grow. In my legal practice I helped small businesses begin by incorporating or forming limited liability companies. I addressed concerns about succession planning for owners who had well-established companies. And I provided advice to clients on handling various issues that they faced in running their businesses. But I also held hands with business owners who were ready to quit because of bad cash flow, employee problems, customer issues, and other frustrations that are all too common.

After closing my legal practice, I formed my own company to provide information to small business owners nationwide. I am a strong believer in the need to continually learn, but recognize that business owners have limited time to devote to this endeavor. My company works to boil down important information and provide resources to help in various aspects of running a business. We've garnered numerous awards for our content and are trusted advisors in the small business community. But we also have multiple revenue streams to ensure that there is always money coming in and opportunities for growth.

If you want to grow bigger, you need more than just basics and information updates. You need the advanced insight that *Think Bigger* offers. You need to develop your own strategy on how to grow. I know this personally and professionally. Let me give you two first-hand examples that illustrate the challenges and rewards of trying to grow a business. Many years ago, a couple of friends and I formed a company to provide cleaning services for group homes. It wasn't difficult to find clients because no other company at the time was offering our unique service. Our employees always did good work, but after a couple of years we shut the company down. The reason: We couldn't charge sufficient fees for the work performed to make a good profit. The company never lost money, but the effort involved wasn't worth it. And because of the low pricing necessitated by the industry (commercial cleaning) coupled with the cost of labor (after employment taxes, workers' compensation, and other insurance), there was no way to scale up. This was a tale of failure in growing a business.

Another example was my father's business. After World War II, he (a mechanic) and a partner started a machine shop. Over the years, they were able to grow in several ways. They went from being subcontractors to manufacturing and marketing products. They built a bigger factory as well as expanding to multiple locations. They also formed partnerships with companies in England, Germany, and Japan, and operated worldwide under their company name. Eventually, a small venture capital firm purchased the business and my father retired. This was a tale of success in growing bigger.

What do these two examples tell us? It can be done, but it's not luck or hard work that will make it so. You may have a great idea for a business, created a business model, set your prices, and gone to work. Now the question becomes: how do you get to the next level? If you've started all by yourself, how do you reach the point of hiring employees? If you've got employees, when and how do you attain the scale to justify having managers? Are you positioned to potentially sell your company or a part of it? Here's where this book comes in. Discover important and practical ways to bring in more revenue, hire more people, and become a bigger business. I know it can be done. And if you've already started a business, I know you have the adventurous spirit to go into the unknown despite obstacles and setbacks. You can do it! You need the information that *Think Bigger* provides so you can become bigger.

Barbara Weltman
www.BigIdeasForSmallBusiness.com
@BigIdeas4SB

PREFACE

WHAT IT SAYS on the cover is true, I did grow an accounting business, and after twelve years I did sell one division of my business (the bookkeeping division) for over a million dollars.

I wanted to write a book about this, not necessarily to be known as an author, but just as a guy who cares about the success of other people, and as someone grateful for what I've accomplished. I wanted to get the message out that *this* can also happen for *you!* I'm wired a bit differently than most accountants and I think that has helped me achieve some success in this industry. I have often described myself to others as an "entrepreneur trapped in an accountant's body," and I wanted to encourage others to take risks, and to enjoy the ride as much as the rewards. I wanted to get accountants to start thinking more like entrepreneurs!

For me, it has always been more about the challenge, the achievement, not just the reward or the money. I love the competition—that drives me more than the material stuff. And I want people to think bigger.

I hope my book inspires you to look at your business in a different way.

—Dan Steiner
Richmond, Virginia
July 2020

[1] IDENTIFY YOUR GOALS

WHAT DO YOU WANT?

DETERMINE WHAT YOU WANT, ultimately, from your business. Do you want your business to be a *job*, or do you want it to create wealth? Do you want to have a *cash-out liquidity event* that provides a retirement check, or do you want a nice, steady job? There's nothing wrong with either one of those paths, but this book is for people who want to run a successful business, grow it, and potentially sell it for a lot of money. That's what you've got to determine early on.

You may change your mind of what you want ten times or a hundred times. I know I have. Any entrepreneur will tell you nothing is set in stone. The joke about me is that I'm capable of changing my mind before I finish a sentence! I have pivoted many times on the direction I was going to take my business. That coupled with every day being both a challenge and an opportunity is what's exciting about owning your own business. Wondering "What's on the other end of that new email that just came in?" Whether the news is good or bad, you get to make impactful decisions on a daily basis – you get to drive! I absolutely love knowing each day is unique and it is never boring.

That's the fun and uniqueness of owning your own business, but with that fun comes lots of challenges and you have to be mentally prepared for both. You can't get too high and you can't get too low or you'll burn out.

Psychology plays as much a role in being a business owner as anything, and not everybody's built for it. There's nothing wrong with wanting to simply run a small bookkeeping business (or any business), where you're the only employee, making $50,000 to $60,000 a year. Even if this is the case, you might still take something out of this book because we're talking about topics that relate to all businesses, even if you want to stay small. But, ultimately, I decided to write this book because I want to challenge you to think bigger!

OWNING YOUR OWN BUSINESS is not a decision to be taken lightly. In fact, it's a BIG decision. With me, I've always been the entrepreneurial type. Growing up, if you're familiar with the 1980s television show, *Family Ties*, I was Alex Keaton (played by Michael J. Fox), the high school student who carried around a briefcase and read the *Wall Street Journal*. That was me.

My parents instilled a work ethic in me from a young age. By the age of 12, I was cutting grass for neighbors and had a couple of newspaper routes (one in the morning and one in the afternoon). My parents were borrowing cash *from me!* When I needed more money to buy something (like a car), I would grab things from around the house and hold yard sales. I was always entrepreneurial. I was fortunate to have worked for very entrepreneurial people during my corporate career and learned a lot (I learned what *to do* and what *not to do*), but I ultimately got frustrated working for other people and helping *them* get rich while I was kept "behind the scenes." I always wanted a seat at the table!

One day I came across Robert Kiyosaki's book, *Rich Dad Poor Dad* and it had a big impact on me. I couldn't put the book down. Once I read that book, I was inspired to go out on my own. I was tired of working a JOB (Just Over Broke) for somebody else and I was willing to take the risks involved. I just needed ideas as to what to do, something I could do with my background and experience that could make a direct impact in people's lives. I scoured Craigslist and saw a bunch of ads for bookkeeping help. I particularly noticed a lot of them were for part-time, hourly bookkeepers, not full-time bookkeeper jobs. I saw right away there was a need in the market.

At the time, back in 2006, outsourcing was not as popular as it is today. Small business owners either did the bookkeeping themselves or tried to hire somebody off Craigslist, and the people you found on Craigslist were usually stay-at-home moms or retired accountants. The alternative was to go to a CPA firm, and CPA firms were (and are) very expensive.

I knew there was a niche to be filled that CPA firms were not going after, and I also knew Craigslist bookkeepers weren't the most professional, had limited capacity, and had limited skillsets. I knew right away I had the formula for a viable business, so I started my company, Steiner Business Solutions, and utilizing the tools and methods outlined in this book, created a very successful and valuable asset for me and my family.

OPPORTUNITY ABOUNDS

I want to help you if you're a $50,000-a-year business, a $200,000-a-year business, or a half-a-million-dollar-a-year business. I want to explain how you can do better, what systems I used, and how I managed to get through some of the situations I faced. And if you want to cash out and sell your business at its highest value, I will tell you how I did it. If you do decide to end your business, *please, please, please* do not walk away without getting *any* value from what you've built! I hear too many times where people say, "Yeah, I'm going to give up and get a steady job," or "I'm going to retire."

"Where'd your clients go?" I ask.

"I don't know. I just put a letter (or email) out to them and told them I was closing down, and if they'd like to get a referral to another accountant, I'd be happy to give it to them."

My jaw drops because there's value in your business and you're giving it away for NOTHING. There's value in your client list. There are buyers out there who want to buy your business! If you've got a $50,000-a-year business, there are buyers out there for you. But, if you can get your business to a million dollars, or a million-and-a-half dollars of revenue, and most of it is recurring, the buyers are going to line up! So, I encourage you to treat your business as an *asset* and *sell* it when you're ready to exit. There is value there! If you walk away, you're leaving money on the table.

This book is about helping you build a mindset of how you can build value in your business so that when it is time to walk away, you're going to get something in return for all your hard work. In my case, I was fortunate to sell a good portion of my business to another company without giving up my entire company and brand. *Steiner Business Solutions* operates several divisions, including QuickBooks training, Mergers and Acquisitions Advisory Services, Business Consulting, Fractional CFO Services, and Tax Preparation Services. I didn't start with all those divisions. I started with just bookkeeping. Over time, I built them organically as well as through acquisitions. I was eventually approached by a business broker who asked me if I was interested in selling my business (or a portion of it), and I decided to do that.

That's not a common thing in our (bookkeeping) industry. There are lots of consolidations and mergers and acquisitions with CPA firms, but not in the bookkeeping industry. There aren't many *big* liquidity events in bookkeeping companies. Most of them are small. I'm sure there are a few out there approaching the million-dollar range, but I don't know of any that have been acquired for over a million dollars.

The company that bought my bookkeeping division is based out of Boston, Massachusetts. They operate a very technology-driven business model with several big investors backing their growth. I was the very first bookkeeping company they acquired. My entire bookkeeping division was acquired, both my employees and clients. From what the broker told me, they started with a list of 500 firms and whittled it down to 50. Steiner Business Solutions was the one they ultimately chose.

I was approached by a broker because I think they were impressed by a few things: My top line revenue, my volume of recurring revenue (bookkeeping clients who pay me every month), and the fact I had a lot of well-trained professional staff. I had good infrastructure, and clients stayed with me.

There are lots of small bookkeeping operators out there. The *majority* of them are sole proprietors. That one person might service as many as 20 clients and produce about $100,000 to $200,000 in revenue a year, maybe, on their own. Then you might have a three- or four-person bookkeeping firm doing upwards of $400,000 or more a year in revenue. You've then probably got a few successful ones doing even more revenue that are potential acquisition targets but, by and large, the *mergers and acquisitions* (M&A) activity in bookkeeping is very small.

I believe this is due to several reasons. Generally speaking, accountants are not big risk-takers. They are not entrepreneurs. Most don't look at a bookkeeping business and say, "Wow, I can turn that into a multimillion-dollar business and then cash out for a couple of million dollars when I'm ready to retire!" They don't think that big. This book, however, is to let you know that it's *possible*, that you can start with no clients and grow to a multimillion-dollar business with several hundred clients, multiple revenue streams, and even multiple divisions. It's possible!

I hope this encourages you to *think bigger*! I want you to think in terms of creating and building a *salable* business. If all you need is a blueprint, that's what this book provides. You will see this *can* happen, and in fact it did (to me!).

[2] How Do I Get IDEAL Clients?

Ask

G ETTING CLIENTS IS ALWAYS a challenge and stress point for any business owner. Getting IDEAL clients is an even bigger challenge. We all wish we could just open our doors and people would start coming in, but we all know that's not going to happen. So, the easy and immediate answer to, "How do I get the right clients?" is *ask*. Many accountants and bookkeepers are introverts. They're very smart people, but they don't consider themselves salespeople. Sales almost has a negative connotation to them and they get embarrassed to ask for business.

I was that person. Growing up I was a fairly shy person, never had a sales job. I was usually in an office environment, sitting at a desk, with not a lot of interaction with the public. Fortunately, as my career advanced, I got a lot more exposure—still never did sales, but worked with a lot of customers, vendors, and key decision-makers, so I got very comfortable being "on the stage."

I think to be good in sales you've got to have *confidence* in what you're selling.

Usually when business owners hit a wall, it's because they don't know how to speak to people about their business, they don't know how to speak about themselves, they don't know what problems they're trying to solve. So, in trying to promote their business, they talk to their friends and family, almost exclusively. These people are easy to approach, what we call *low hanging fruit*. It's definitely a great place to start getting the word out and working on your "pitch", but you have to realize that you can't grow a successful business simply relying on friends and family.

RESEARCH

I consistently research my competition and I stay involved in my local business community. I encourage you to sign up for all your local small business email blasts. There are a lot of small business media sources that produce newsletters which come out every day. You need to be reading those. You need to get as many articles, newsletters, business postings, and media sources as you can, locally. Read them and find out what's going on in your market, who's working where, who's moving, who's buying who. Many of your ideal clients will appear in the news and you now have some background information to use when you reach out to them about your company.

PASSION

Growing up, I was pretty introverted. I had a lot of friends, but I wasn't very chatty or looking to hang out with people all the time. Once I started my business, I had to become much more extroverted. I tell people even today, if I go to a party with friends or to some kind of social setting, I'm not the one going around striking up conversations. I'll probably get a drink and go sit at a table where there's not a lot of people sitting. That's me, personally.

But when you get me talking about my business, watch out! I'm so passionate about what I do that I can't stop talking about it. That's the mindset you have to have. This is your baby. If you're not inspired by what you do and who you serve, that comes across to the person on the other side of that conversation. Business owners need to feel your passion. They need to know you're authentic and that your interests are their interests. They need to see you want to help them solve their problems.

I'm so competitive and passionate about what my company did for business owners that I wanted to tell everybody, and you couldn't shut me up. I mean, I could talk for hours and hours about what I do. I know my clients. I know the small business owner very well. Not just because I work with them, but because *I'm one of them.*

This should be a passionate thing because you have to believe that what you're doing serves a greater good and that the success of your clients' is going to create success in your business.

CLIENT NEEDS

Being a business owner, you have to understand people and relate to them at all levels. Business owners come in all forms, shapes, sizes, education levels, backgrounds, personalities—you name it. In preparing for new client meetings, you can't use the same pitch on every business owner. You kind of gauge and understand who it is you're talking to and figure out where their *pain points* are. They don't want you to just read off a list of everything you do in your business.

I always ask clients, "What do you think you need?" "What are your goals?" They often don't know what they need, but if I get them talking about their business, I'm going to find opportunities where I can help them. And that's what they would rather discuss with you, anyway. They need to see you didn't just come to brag about all the different things you do. They need to see you have a genuine interest in them, and that you have a genuine interest in their business.

After you listen to them tell you about their business and their challenges, come back with, "You know what, you mentioned that you're not getting your financial statements in a timely manner. Well, we recognize that business owners need to have timely and accurate financial statements so they can make sound business decisions. Did you know we guarantee you're going to get your financial statements every month with our monthly bookkeeping package, and you're going to get a profit and loss statement and a balance sheet every single month?"

Those are the types of interactions you need to have. You need to have empathy for your client and understand what their needs are and address those specific needs. You'll have time to tell them about your other services but, ultimately, you want to deliver a solution to what the small business owner needs.

SOCIAL MEDIA

By and large, Facebook hasn't done a lot for me. While there are some decent Facebook bookkeeping groups out there you can join and use if you've got questions about your bookkeeping business, I have not found that Facebook generates new business. If you post content on Facebook, you're going to have to "boost" it (paid advertising) to get any sort of audience for the post. Even with paid advertising I haven't seen good results and I don't see or hear of many business owners who go to Facebook to find a bookkeeper or accountant for their business. You can have a Facebook business page (it doesn't cost anything) but I would use that more for branding than I would for business development.

With Twitter it's kind of the same thing—I haven't gotten any business, really, off of Twitter, either. I do post content on Twitter, but again, it's more for branding and keeping my name out there. In fact, for generating leads, Twitter is probably worse than Facebook.

For professional service companies, I think LinkedIn is the place to be. But you can't just build a profile on LinkedIn and think everything's going to be fine. You also can't just have 600 connections on LinkedIn and think everything's going to be fine. At the end of the day, I'm looking for *referrals*. You need to post content there constantly. If you meet someone at a networking event, you should follow up with them on LinkedIn. Don't let that opportunity go to waste.

I have also used LinkedIn as a way to prepare for meetings. If I knew I was going to meet with a new business lead, I would always look that business owner up on LinkedIn, look up their company's website, and make sure I knew as much about the owner and the company as I could before I went into the meeting. Then after the meeting (or at times even before the meeting), I would send a connection request to the owner.

Before meeting, if someone wants to check you out, they aren't necessarily going to ask you for your resume, but they're probably going to look up your profile on LinkedIn. So, I make it easy for them. I send them a connection request, and then they can check me out and look at all my history, look at articles I've posted, and they can see all the recommendations I have on LinkedIn. It was a good way to promote myself very easily without having to run my mouth for 20 minutes!

WORKING REFERRALS

Referrals are arguably the best source of your ideal clients. As an accountant, you want to network with bankers, lawyers, insurance agents—basically people who also routinely interact with business owners. Everybody needs an accountant, but you want to find people in your network who deal with your IDEAL client. I learned early on there are *influencers* in your business community, people who seem to be known by everyone. These are the folks that show up at every chamber event, every networking event. They've been in your town for years and years. They're the blue bloods. I always went after hungry people like myself who I knew were trying to build a book of business and were looking for referral partners like I was.

I would say, "Hey, are you currently referring anybody out for bookkeeping work or tax work?"

And if they said, "No, I'm kind of just getting started," that would be a good connection opportunity.

Those are the people I would target because if I went to someone who has been around town forever, and knows everybody already, they are already referring business to other accountants and CPAs. I did not want to waste time on trying to build up a relationship that wouldn't deliver any referrals for me (or them, really). That doesn't mean I didn't spend *some* time telling them about my business. I never walked away from a chance to promote! I just didn't invest a lot of time.

In a nutshell, you want to establish just a handful of people who are going to be interacting with your type of ideal client and try to be either the first or second resource they send referrals to. I always wanted to be *first,* of course, but that's a lot to ask of somebody, so I'd follow up with, "Well, at least let me be number two!"

I would then work that relationship deep. I would meet with that person once a week over coffee and really get them involved in what I was doing. And I always tried to do business with them, too. A referral partnership means you're referring business back. When you're networking with people it should not just be a one-way relationship because that will be the reputation you get. "I send work to Dan all the time and that guy never sends anything back to me." In which case they more than likely might stop sending me work if nothing is in it for them. So make sure to repay that person with referrals from you.

Put in the time and effort and keep your eyes open to refer business back to your referral partners or that resource is going to dry up, eventually. It's *work*. Ultimately, getting new clients is *hard work*. And you can't do it by yourself. You have to have other people putting the word out there. That's what you get through LinkedIn and through using your network of business contacts. But just think about how many new clients you're going to get, if you work things this way, and create the possibility of exponential networking. The more people you add to your network, the more referrals you're going to get.

If you're thinking, *Well, I work with a couple people and they send me some clients*, that's fine, but if two people are sending you that many clients, what if you had five people sending you that many clients? What if you have 10 people sending you that many clients? Simply stated, put the work in and look for networking opportunities.

Then go deep with them. There are so many people on LinkedIn who have *brush-by* relationships with their connections, and it's hard to refer people if you don't really know them. I'm very uncomfortable just giving out names of people I don't really know. Giving referrals is part of your *brand* and if you send somebody a bad referral, that's going to reflect poorly on you and your reputation is going to get muddied. So, it's very important you value and treasure these referral partners you're going to work with.

PROFESSIONAL NETWORKS

How do you find these referral partners? One resource available is your local Chamber of Commerce. They are constantly holding social and business events where you can meet other business owners. For me, I started off using BNI (Business Network International, www.bni.com), which is an international networking organization. When I started scouring all the BNI groups in Richmond, I looked for BNI groups that were just forming because most of the established groups already had an accountant member.

When we started that group, we probably had 10 people in it. After a couple years, there were probably 30+ people in that group. That meant I had *exclusive access to promote my business with 29 other business owners*. Every week at the meetings I stood up in front of the group and introduced myself and my business and asked for referrals. The group really coached me to be a good networker and it produced enough new business to help launch my young company.

Odds are you're not going to get referrals from 29 people. But it's the same strategy I mentioned earlier, which is to *find a few people and really deep dive and build relationships with those people*. So, within a group of 29, I would find three to five people I just seem to gel with. Whether they were in industries that specifically worked with my type of client or not, I identified them as potentially strong referral partners. In the bulk of my time working in that group, I worked mostly with those three or four same people.

Now, I saw all 29 people every week, and I still networked with them, but I would do it at a very high level. I would do five minutes here, five minutes there. Just getting caught up on their current events. There are plenty of networking groups out there. BNI is the one that I'm most familiar with.

It's a sign of success when your book of business is generating leads for you. You don't have to go out there and attend all these networking functions anymore, or as much. During the first couple years after I started Steiner Business Solutions, I was going to as many networking events as I could find. I was trying to meet as many people as I could meet but, ultimately, you've got to get disciplined and focused and you can't be wasting time.

As a business owner, your time is everything. You're going to get inundated with people who want to network with you. You're going to get inundated with people who tell you they can help you and they've got a ton of business to refer you. Well, you'll get smarter and smarter about that. And the longer you're in business, you're going to be able to flush those people out immediately. You're going to learn who you should talk to and who you shouldn't.

Your network *needs to work for you.* Your network is a piece of your marketing arm. Your network is the source of some of your best testimonials that you're going to need. So, it's critical that you leverage your network.

CLIENTS LEAD TO BETTER CLIENTS

It took me years to develop who I thought was my ideal client. Look at clients as necessary cash infusion, but also look at them as an educational opportunity. Your early clients are the ones that are going to help you form the policies of your business. And there's nothing like a real-time case study to figure out or refine your business model. I still have clients who stayed with me for years and years but others, they fell by the wayside. They were great initially and I learned a lot from them but, ultimately, as I grew my business, I found they weren't the right fit for me. But I didn't know that until I worked with them. Now, I can be very selective with the clients I work with, which allows me higher profit margins and satisfying work.

PAID AND FORMAL REFERRAL PROGRAMS

We talked about using your *network* but when I say referral *programs*, some of those might be paid referral programs. I had referral programs with employees. I would offer incentives to my staff if they were able to bring in new client leads. They didn't have to close the lead or do the proposal, but they did bring me the leads. I would also run referral programs for my existing clients. You want to encourage your existing clients to refer you to their friends and other business owners because business owners hang out with business owners. You especially want your IDEAL clients referring their colleagues because, more than likely, they will turn out to be IDEAL clients as well. With such programs, you only pay out if you get a referral client, so it's money well spent.

Which brings us back to my very first point, which was you don't get a new client unless you *ask* for a new client. So, you can have a referral program and you can post it on your website, you can send out letters to your clients, you can do all the things you think you should do to let everybody know that you have a referral program, but that's not going far enough. You need to talk to your clients. You should be talking to your clients frequently, and it never hurts to ask before you hang up the phone for a referral.

Ask your clients if there is anybody else in their network of business owners who are facing struggles with their bookkeeping? Are they happy with their CPA? You should not be embarrassed to ask for that. Your clients need to be reminded that you are looking for new business. The clients have enough issues of their own in what they have to deal with in their own businesses, so they are not always thinking about sending you referrals, it's not at the top of their list. So, it's important that you remind them when you do talk to them:

"Are you happy with what we do for you? You are? Great. Is there anybody in your network who you think would be a great fit for us? I would love to be introduced!"

You have to ask. You can't assume that people are out there referring you to everybody they know. It'd be great if they did and there might be some that are but it's critical that you are constantly reminding them you are looking for more business and you would appreciate their help. It's important you develop formal referral programs for employees and your existing clients.

FORMER COLLEAGUES

Another good resource for getting clients are former employers and co-workers. Many of the people you used to work with have probably left your former company and might be in a position at another company now where they can influence who does the accounting work. It's important to keep in touch with people you used to work with, particularly if you worked with somebody at a CPA firm or another accounting firm. Typically, those people are going to stay in the industry. And people you may have worked with at whatever level, may have been promoted either within the same company or at a different company where they're now the decision-maker on who does the accounting work—whether they do it in-house or outsource it.

So, stay in touch with people you used to work with (LinkedIn is a great way to accomplish this.) because you never know where they're going to end up. That just gives you more opportunities to get your foot in the door in some of these other businesses.

Your former employer could be one of your best clients. Think of that. I've had people I've hired as employees for my company, and one of the first things I'll ask them is, "Okay, I'm getting ready to hire you away from your employer. Do you think they would be open to having you work for them, through me?" Her or his former employer might be a new client of mine. And now this person is going to be their bookkeeper again, but through *my company!*

There's a lot of opportunity with former employers, whether it's your previous employer you left to start your own business or any number of prior employers you used to work for. They already know and trust you—two big obstacles you typically face with new clients, are already overcome. That sounds like an ideal client.

THE SECRET

At the end of the day, you have got to be authentic. You have to believe in what you're doing. It's not always about being the smartest. I don't ever think I'm the smartest person in the room, but people know I genuinely care about their business and I spend the time to learn about their business. And that approach is going to help you get the clients you want. When it's not an IQ test, I think it comes down to personality. And I think the majority of my success in getting new clients was my personality and how I approached each new conversation. If you just go in reading a pitch, using talking points, and you don't mix it up and blend in your own personality, you're going to struggle. You're going to be just like all the rest.

- Use your *personality* and your *passion* to your advantage because that is the differentiating factor. We're all created individually. We're not cloned. Use what makes you special to get clients. Use your individuality to your advantage. If you do what everybody else is doing and you're just bland in the way you approach people, you're not going to be as successful. Use your personality, be authentic, be empathetic, and be passionate about what your business can do for people and you will get the opportunity.

- Don't be afraid to *ask* those you trust and respect to refer you to their network of business owners.
- And *hustle*. I never, to this day, stop thinking about how I can grow my business, how I can get new, high value clients.

Getting new clients is all about your *mindset*. With everyone you meet, it has to be foremost in your mind, it has to be, *How can I help that person? Is there an opportunity for me in my business to help that person?"*

And to figure out if you can help that person, you have to *talk* to that person, and you have to understand them and their business. Once you get past that part, the sales part is easy. I never put any sales pressure on myself. The pressure is to just be *you*, just be natural and the "sales part" will come naturally. People who think they're being *sold to* are not going to sign up with you. People don't like to be sold to. It's important you simply have *conversations* with people and they don't even feel they're being sold.

That's the secret, just have a conversation. Once they learn about what you can do for them, you don't need to sell them.

[3] MARKETING, MESSAGING, BRANDING

T HIS CHAPTER ON MARKETING, messaging, and branding is probably my favorite section of the book. I have always loved marketing my business. Since day one, I've been very involved in the process and I am even to this day.

You have to treat your business as an investment, as an asset. If you just look at this as a job, you lose sight of a lot of value. And since day one, I've always treated my company as a *brand*. I mean, Steiner Business Solutions has my name on it. When I first started thinking about the name of my company, I had a lot of people advise me, "Well, you probably shouldn't put your name in it, for your own protection. And if you ever want to expand, other people might not want to have Steiner in the name." But at the end of the day, I decided this company was about *my* mission and *my* personality, and I've never looked back.

BRANDING

To me, your brand is the most important asset you have, even when you put it up against your book of business. The clients I had accumulated were there because of the way we treated them, and because of the positive results they received, within the care of *my brand*. When my bookkeeping division was acquired, part of the value they saw in me was my brand.

You hear the saying, "You only get one opportunity to make a good first impression." That has stuck with me since the beginning. Really put some thought into what you want your company to be about and what image does it portray to the outside world—more importantly to potential clients, and ultimately to a potential BUYER. Consider carefully who you're looking to serve (i.e. IDEAL client), along with your mission and your passion.

From day one everything you do either helps or hurts your brand. You have to protect that at all costs. Think of it is as a child. As a parent, we would do anything to protect our children. That's the same mentality you need to have for your business. Through all the years, my staff made plenty of mistakes. I certainly didn't enjoy those mistakes, and we tried to limit our mistakes, but at the same time, I didn't get very upset about them. The things I would get upset about, however, included actions where an employee did something I thought would damage our brand. "If you want to see Dan get upset, do something that could negatively impact his reputation or brand in the community," they'd say.

In those instances, as an employee of mine, that's when you ran the risk of losing your job because there was no second-guessing, there was no indecision if it impacted my brand. It didn't matter how little or small the infraction was. The issue was handled swiftly and decisively.

If a client said, "I don't think you guys delivered on your services," I wasn't going to argue with them. If they wanted their money back, I didn't hesitate. I'd give them their money back. I didn't want anyone to think we were trying to take advantage of anybody, we were trying to get over on anybody, or that we had any dishonest business practices going on with my company. If any of my clients expressed even a hint of thinking we were dishonest or doing something we shouldn't have been doing, I'd nip that in the bud quickly. I would get involved.

I would talk to my employees and get to the bottom of any issue. Even though we were usually right, or we had proof that something was done correctly, or we did everything we could in good faith, I still wasn't going to get into an argument with the client and I would immediately refund them their money because I knew that a $600 refund back to the client was worth it because it protected my brand. I didn't want that client spreading the word that my company was dishonest or doing something they shouldn't have done. That was not worth fighting over $500 or $600.

Any time a decision had to be made of whether to do something or not do something, it always came back to "Well, how does this impact my brand?" I can't stress this enough. You should consider your brand in every decision you make. And part of that, obviously, is in the way you conduct yourself, in the way your employees conduct themselves, in the culture that you are building with your company. That's all part of your brand.

MARKETING

Let's talk a little bit about marketing. I believe you should start early. A lot of business owners bootstrap and think, "Well, I don't have the money to invest in a whole lot of marketing."

You need to look at marketing as not just an overhead item, it's not just a line item on your P&L. You should always feel like you're getting a return on your marketing dollars. And that's where I struggled, quite honestly, when I first started getting into marketing. My frustration was that I was spending a lot of money and not getting a lot of clients from it.

But there are two ways of marketing—there's the *branding* type of marketing which includes coming up with your logo, your color scheme, your slogan or tagline, your website, the optics of what your business looks like.

And then there's the *call to action* type of marketing which you should be doing more analytics on.

In the early years of my business I was putting a lot of pressure on my branding dollars to give me some sort of return or analytics, and you just can't do that. You have to invest in your branding over time, as it's a slower return on investment. You certainly want a clean look, you want your branding to be easy to understand, you want to look professional, but don't think you're going to get an immediate return on your investment. Don't put that kind of stress on it because it's not going to happen. But you need to do it, nonetheless.

The biggest marketing investment I made (and continue to make) is my website. I came out of the gate with a very professional looking website and that has delivered great results for me—not just with branding, but it has delivered new clients to my doorstep as well. You absolutely need to have a website in some form or fashion.

For whatever reason, I still see accountants, bookkeepers, and CPAs who don't! It's astonishing to me. If you want to compete at all in today's market, *you've got to have a website*. How much you invest in it is up to you. As I said, I did invest a lot of my early capital into a very nice professional website. And I know that got me business.

If somebody gave out three referrals for accounting firms, mine being one of them, and if two of the referrals didn't have a website and I did, I had a much better chance of getting that client than the other two. I knew that was one of the ways I was going to distinguish myself. I tried to be forward thinking in everything I did, and I knew that I needed to have a website if I was going to compete.

You should take a very involved role in your marketing. Don't just hand it off to somebody and give them free will to do what they want to do. Don't give them an unlimited budget. Secondly, they're putting the image out there of *you*. I wouldn't let anyone put messaging out unless I approved it first. I had to sign off on everything before it got published. Even to this day, nothing hits the public's eye unless I approve it. I've just made that the way I do business, and I recommend it.

Again, your brand is your most important asset. Hold your marketing vendors accountable. They sometimes look for easy ways out, for quick fixes. "What do you think of this? We like this image," they might say. Don't just quickly approve these things. My marketing people will tell you I critique every image that goes on our website, on our brochure, whatever. I have an idea of what I want, and until I get what I want, it doesn't get published. So, be passionate, be disciplined, be involved in everything that goes out to the public that's got your name on it all throughout your entire business—even when you get big and you've got managers who work for you. Even if I had an internal marketing person, I'm sure I would still want to approve everything before it went out.

This is my advice, whether you're good at marketing, bad at marketing, it doesn't matter. I've never claimed to be the creative type. I certainly don't come up with all the creative work that has been done for my business, but I certainly know what image I'm trying to project. I certainly know what messaging I want to put out. I know the direction that I want to go. It's so critical I don't leave that up to other people.

AWARDS

Worth mentioning are some of the awards Steiner Business Solutions has won. In Richmond, the local newspaper (*Richmond Times Dispatch*) grants awards to local businesses every year. They call them the RTD Best Awards. The backstory is these awards have been going on for years. There are 50 or so categories that you can win as the Best of Richmond. There is also recognition for the two runners-up in each category. I was approached by the *Times Dispatch* one year and they said, "Hey, Dan, we'd love for you to be an advertiser in these RTD Best Awards."

"Well," I said, "I'm surprised I don't see a category for accounting firms."

"You're right. That's interesting," said the woman I was dealing with.

"Well, you want me to advertise in something that doesn't even have my category and I just don't feel good about that," I said.

"I agree with you," she said.

She went and talked to whomever was in charge of that program at the newspaper and the next year they ended up adding *accounting firm* as a "best of" category. I am a strong advocate for my industry, and I'm proud to say my company won *Best Accounting Firm in Richmond, Virginia*, the very first year the award was given!

We have also been recognized by another local media outlet, in a program called the "Rising 25." Every year they ask companies to submit their tax returns over a three-year period and they produce a list of the top 25 companies in Richmond who have had the most growth in revenue over that period of time. I've made that list the last three years in a row!

Awards and achievements—It's nice to have these play a part in the marketing and branding of your business.

Me holding my first Rising 25 plaque

& Harrison. They take on personal injury cases, Social Security disability benefits and Virginia Worker's Compensation benefits.

First Runner Up
Allen, Allen, Allen & Allen

Second Runner Up
Hairfield Morton

The Best Local Accounting Firm

Winner
Steiner Business Solutions
8814 Fargo Road, #225, Richmond
804-525-4259
steinerbusinesssolutions.com

From accounting to taxes to QuickBooks training and everything in between, you can rely on Steiner to provide quality services for your small business. Their friendly, knowledgeable team elevates number-crunching to an art with insightful advice and round-the-clock accessibility.

First Runner Up
Keiter CPAs

Second Runner Up
Adams, Jenkins & Cheatham

The Best Local Financial Services Firm

Winner
Virginia Credit Union
Visit the website for Richmond locations
vacu.org

"RTD Best" Award Winner!

Image © 2020 Dan Steiner

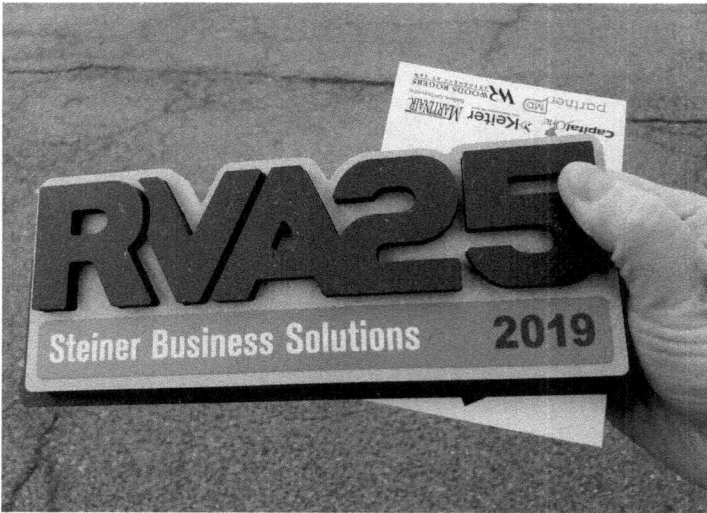

Rising 25 – 2nd Year
Image © 2020 Dan Steiner

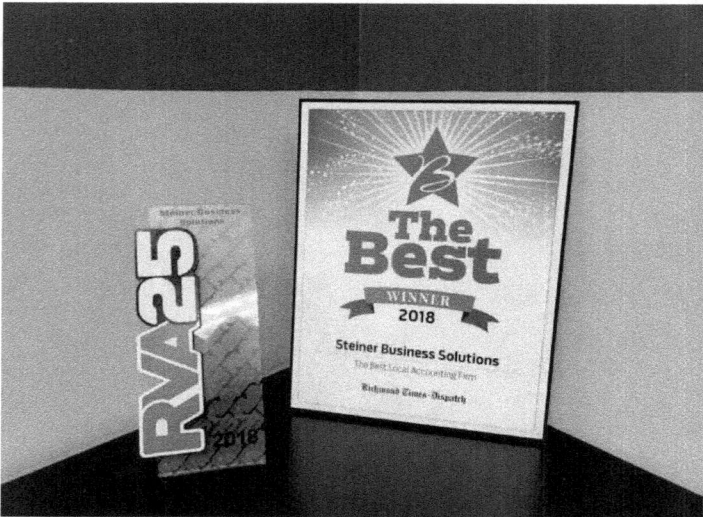

Local Awards on Display at the Office
Image © 2020 Dan Steiner

I don't do traditional advertising. I don't do newspaper ads, TV, or radio. I've always tried to be that company people *hear about in conversations and read about in testimonials*. We've gotten a lot of our business through referrals. It's still important you promote that you're successful and certainly that's reflected in these awards. It's one way we stand out in a crowded field.

With these awards, people saw our name. People saw we were a growing company. It didn't cost me anything and it was good publicity. With the RTD Best Awards we won it says, "Best Local Accounting Firm." Well, guess what? I'm going to capitalize on that by putting that "phrase" in all my marketing materials and bring it up in every conversation, "Hey, did you know we were voted the Best Local Accounting Firm in Richmond, Virginia?" Does that mean we *were* the best local accounting firm? Heck no. I mean, there are plenty of qualified, smart, accounting firms out there, but none of them could say they were voted the Best Local Accounting Firm! We just outsmarted them and outhustled them this time. So, I took advantage of these opportunities to stand out from the crowd.

In fact, the year we won the award, the runner-up was one of the best-known, one of the most high-powered, wealthiest accounting firms in Richmond. They came in second place behind little old Steiner Business Solutions! Honestly, I still can't wipe the smile off my face when I think about it. That award really put us on the map. The good press I got out of winning that one award was mammoth. It's critical small business owners don't just sit on the sidelines. Look for opportunities to promote yourself that will distinguish you from the others. Awards are good for business; they bring credibility to your brand.

SOCIAL MEDIA

I do think social media can be effective in certain aspects of marketing. I see it as quasi-*branding*, but also a *call to action* marketing tool. It hasn't worked well for Steiner Business Solutions, though. I have invested time and money in doing it, and I've concluded for professional service firms like ours, it's challenging trying to get clients through social media. People don't necessarily arrive at the trust level needed to hire a professional service firm from social media. That said, I have used social media for branding when I want to put *content* out there. The key to branding, the key to lead generation through social media, is you have to have content. You just can't sit on the sidelines and expect business owners are going to find you.

I get email newsletters from five or six different sources every day, probably more than that. Some are industry-specific newsletters, some are local newspapers, some are other small business media outlets. I comb through those every day. If I see an article that I think is relevant to my clients or small business owners, I'll share that article on all my social media platforms. I use Twitter, Facebook, and of course, LinkedIn. I don't use Instagram but that's pretty popular now.

You have to keep your name out there. The more articles you post, the more your credibility grows. Your perception of being an expert grows. Small business owners appreciate that you're taking the time to help them out. When I share content, I'm not asking for them to sign up as a client, I'm just trying to help educate them. So, content is key. You want to do it constantly through social media but also update the content on your website. Your website should stay fresh. Don't let the same content sit there for too long. That's very common if you look at many websites, unfortunately, but that's not good for business. It's not good for search engine optimization, either.

What's going to keep a client coming back? If a client comes to your website and they gobble up all content you have, then they come back 60 days later and find the same articles, they're not going to come back to your website again. You want *return visitors* to your website. It's great if they come once— that's better than nothing, but you want business owners to visit your website often because they find *new* content helpful for them and they begin to look at you as an expert in your field. That will generate business! It's important you work with your marketing vendor on this, although a lot of the content posted I did myself.

I still, to this day, manage all my social media accounts. It's not hard and they're free. I coach clients to do all the free things at your disposal. If you're not maxing out on every free social media outlet, free marketing, free anything, then I don't think you're going to be as successful as you can be. I would come home and post content on all my social media. It cost me a little bit of time, but it didn't cost me any money. It's a way to get your name out, a way to brand yourself, and to increase your credibility at no cost. Even though I don't believe social media has given me an immediate ROI, I think it has helped with my brand. It helps keep me focused, it forces me to produce content.

The key takeaway is you want to keep your content fresh so people are coming back to you regularly, until they are ready to reach out for your services.

SEO

Other than our website, one of the best investments I ever made in my marketing was in *search engine optimization*, called SEO. You could have the best looking website out there, but if nobody finds it, it's a sunk cost. It's worthless. Unless you specifically send someone to your website (for example, sending them a link), without SEO people are not going to find you.

With SEO, you really do need to work with people who know what they're talking about because keywords are tricky. You might think your clients are searching for certain keywords when they're not. You'd be surprised at some of the weirdest, oddest, strangest phrases and keywords that people search on Google to find your type of service. Talk to somebody who is an expert or skilled in SEO and tell them, "Look, I want to be on page one of bookkeeping services in my town or my city. I want to be number one and I want you to get me there." I am fortunate that I found talented people who have managed my SEO campaigns for me, with awesome results. One of those people is Patrick McFadden, owner of Indispensable Marketing in Richmond, Virginia. Patrick has worked with me for years, so I asked him to write on this topic in *Think Bigger*. His contribution is in the back of the book under Appendix A. Feel free to contact Patrick if you would like help with YOUR search engine optimization.

Early on you're going to pay more for SEO because you're just starting out and you have to build the right content (keywords and phrases) on your website. It's going to take time for SEO to kick in, but once it does, you or your marketing people won't have to spend nearly as much time to keep you up there. And once you're up there, the maintenance is a whole lot less expensive.

At first, we focused on bookkeeping SEO. As I created my QuickBooks training division, we built an SEO campaign around QuickBooks training. Eventually we were ranked number one in QuickBooks training. You want SEO to work for you. You want it to drive the *right traffic* to your website. Don't just have a website. If you're not paying for SEO along with your website, you're not going to get any or much return from your website.

SALESPEOPLE

Should I hire a salesperson?

That's a good question. I have hired salespeople for other businesses I was involved in. It didn't work out, and I've never hired a salesperson for Steiner Business Solutions. At the end of the day, *I'm* the best salesperson for my business. And you, as the business owner, *you* should be the best salesperson. You might say, "Look, I'm not a good salesperson. I don't have the personality. I don't enjoy doing sales. But as the owner, you *have* to force yourself to become the best salesperson you can be. Your survival depends upon it!

Do not go out and hire a bunch of salespeople. I've seen that happen in some of my clients' businesses. They immediately invest a lot of money in salespeople. Remember, *these are salespeople.* They're going to tell you they could sell anything. They're going to promise you all these great results. They're going to say, "I'm going to bring in so much business you're going to have to knock them away with a stick." Well, I can tell you from my experience, you may find *one* who can get measurable results, but only after you've worked with 10 of them who didn't get squat. Not many small business owners I know can afford to go through that exercise.

I got to the point where my business was generating so much referral business, my website was generating so many leads, my SEO was generating so many leads, that I didn't need to hire a salesperson. Think about that. Take the money you budgeted for a salesperson and invest it in your infrastructure. All the money I spent on SEO, all the money I spent on the website, all the time I spent developing my network of referrals, that was a fraction of what you would spend on a salesperson.

I'm not saying you should *never* hire a salesperson because I'm sure it works for some people. I would say don't make that decision too early. You should be the number one salesperson for the entire existence of your company but at some point, if you feel like you've got other things to focus on, and your business can afford a salesperson, and you're willing to invest some money to see *if* you can find somebody who is going to help your growth, then that's fine.

My website is a great salesperson. My network of contacts is my sales team. Why do I want to bring on another employee who may or may not do a good job?

More than anything, *you* should be your best salesperson. If you aren't going out there and selling your business, if you're going to leave it up to someone who doesn't have your passion, doesn't know your business, doesn't know your clients, you're going to be disappointed. To get clients, people have to know you're authentic. And I think a client would rather do business when they're sitting across the table from the business owner versus a salesperson. I've gotten many clients because they knew they were talking to the business owner. There's a lot of faith and trust and belief in that. If they're sitting across the table from a salesperson, it doesn't carry the same weight.

MESSAGING

Your messaging should deliver your ideal clients. When you first started out, you probably weren't as picky about the clients you worked with. But you sure did learn a lot of lessons from them.

Hopefully you learned enough from them that they've helped you define your ideal client. This, will in turn, help you define and target the right messaging for your business. With your messaging, everything you do, whether it's on a business card, a website, a brochure, or a sales flyer, you want to deliver the right message. Part of that messaging is about branding, but it's also about *solving problems*. You don't want your messaging to be about how great you are. You want it to be about how you solve problems.

How can you make that business owner's life less stressful? The service you provide can make that business owner more money or help them sleep at night.

Even though you want to build your credibility, your messaging should also be helping you *qualify leads*. An online FAQ page is a perfect example of how we prequalify folks and how you get your messaging across. We want to preemptively put out there some of the questions people are going to be asking, and we give them the answers right there on the website. This way, when they read those questions and answers, they can decide, "Okay, based on what they're saying, I don't think this is the right fit for me." That saves us the time of having to do that through a free consultation.

It's critical that you constantly work on your messaging. You want it to be brief, concise, and to the point.

TESTIMONIALS

Get plenty of fresh testimonials. Business owners want to hear from other business owners, they don't want to hear from a salesperson. They don't just want to read *your* words on a website. Anybody can say anything on a website or a brochure. So, if you have a business owner or one of your existing clients saying, "Steiner Business Solutions has been great to work with. We're so much more successful. I'm such a better business owner since I've been working with Steiner Business Solutions," that's what carries the weight and the credibility that other owners want to see. They want to see that you solved a problem for that company that this owner has as well. There's some commonality there.

Therefore, you want to put as many case studies on your website or in your marketing materials as you can. You want to show, "Here's an example of an issue this client had, and this is how we solved it," because solving that one problem, you could find 50 business owners in your market who have the exact same problem. If you can showcase how you helped this one client solve that same problem, there's a good chance those 50 other business owners are going to give you a call.

Testimonials are effective. Case studies, testimonials, they're kind of the same thing but you want your clients talking about you. You want your clients promoting you. Some of your best client leads are going to come from your existing clients.

AGAIN . . . ASK!

Again, don't be afraid to ask. Don't be afraid to ask your clients to refer business to you, and don't be afraid to ask them for a testimonial. It could be a video testimonial or a written testimonial. Videos are the more popular way to do that now. I would encourage you to do videos versus anything else but the more you can get your clients talking about you and what problems you solved for them, the greater the dividends you will reap.

One challenge with testimonials early on is that people will refer to *you,* specifically. I was the company. Everybody talked about "Dan." All the testimonials we did the first few years I was in business, we laugh at now because every client mentions my name, not so much Steiner Business Solutions. "Dan helped me with this. Dan is great. Dan is a pleasure to work with. Dan really helped me here."

You really need to convert these people from *you* being the company to the company being its own entity. All the testimonials we get now are about how great Steiner Business Solutions is, how good the team is. That's going to help give the perception of professionalism of your company, and the size of your company. A lot of people say when you start out, you want your company to look as big as it can be, even if it's just you. If it is just you and you're working out of your house, you want the impression when somebody comes to your website to be that you're a good-sized company. Your messaging probably doesn't say it's "just Sally who works from her home office all by herself." No, you talk about *the company.*

They don't know it's just Sally. For all they know, there are 15 employees in your company. I pivoted to that strategy pretty early on because I wanted to compete for more valuable clients. Some of the bigger, high value clients aren't looking for a one-person operation because they're worried about your capacity, quite honestly. If you can give the impression you're bigger than you are, you're probably going to get bigger clients, more sophisticated clients, and you're going to look more professional.

STANDING OUT

How do you stand out? If a small business owner is looking for somebody to work with and they've got five choices, how are you going to be their number one choice? *It is all about perception.* You want to be professional. You want to show credibility. It's critical you build your messaging around that.

What does Dan do when he comes home from work after a long day? He starts working on his marketing. That was very common for me. I probably worked on my marketing three or four nights a week, constantly figuring out what I could do with my marketing. I had full access to my website. When they built my website, I wanted to be able to get in the back door through the admin portal of the site. I wanted to update it, change the wording, change the messaging, I didn't have to send an email to my vendor to do it. I just went in and did it myself.

Those late-night hours were really focused on my marketing and my branding and I can't stress it enough—If you want to have a good exit value when you go to sell your business, your brand and your reputation is the goodwill, they're the x-factor that's going to determine how much you're going to get for your business. So, it's vital that with every decision you make, your branding and your reputation should always factor into every decision.

MARKETING IS VITAL, of course. Everybody bootstraps, and it's amazing how many people spend their money on the wrong things. If I can convince you not to spend it on a salesperson, to invest instead in SEO, for example, that is going to help you get more clients. Just the return on that investment, in my opinion, is huge. Even though bookkeepers and accountants don't generally have a marketing or salesperson mentality or personality, they need to recognize they're going to have to work twice as hard to overcome that challenge. You have got to be able to get your name out there to really grow your business.

[4] PRICING & CONTRACTS

PRICING

PRICING IS A TOUGH TOPIC because everyone's got advice on how you should price. The best advice I can give is that you price your services so you make a profit!

Simple enough, right? That should be the underlying philosophy for all pricing decisions. The caveat there is when you first start out your business, you can't be as sensitive to price. When I left the business world as a W2 employee, I was making a good salary. If you calculated my hourly rate, it was pretty significant. When I started my bookkeeping business full time in 2007, I didn't have a salary. I ate what I killed. I billed my services for $15 an hour. That was certainly, at my level of experience, a significant pay cut, but the purpose of that pricing was twofold:

1. I needed to get in some doors, so I knew I had to price low, even below my true value in order to get new clients.
2. Once I had clients, I needed to build my brand and reputation in the small business community.

I was cheap and that's what a lot of business owners wanted. When I started working for them, they soon realized they had gotten a very skilled professional for $15 an hour, and that helped me build my brand.

It's important you don't have the mindset of, "Well, I've got a college degree," or "I'm a QuickBooks expert," or "I've been working at a CPA firm and I was making $80,000 a year, so I need to charge a fee high enough to at least earn that much income." That thinking doesn't take a lot of thought! When you don't have a strong brand and you don't have a strong reputation, people will be hesitant to pay a higher fee. People who don't know you think there's a lot of risk in hiring you. They will be inclined to pay as little as possible because they don't know you; but mostly because they've never *heard* of you.

That was my initial strategy, to go low, build a client base, and then I raised my prices after I'd established a brand and a name and some credibility in the market. *That doesn't mean I was losing money* because when you're starting out by yourself, as the owner and sole proprietor, you're at 100% gross profit. You're not paying anybody but yourself. If you had to turn around and pay somebody else $12 an hour to do that $15 an hour work, obviously, that's very little gross profit. After you throw in some overhead costs, you might not be making any money.

Pricing strategy is much more flexible when you're a sole proprietor. Your overhead structure should be easier to manage and control, so you are able to manipulate your pricing in order to accelerate your business' growth.

As you grow and you get more clients, you can start to raise your prices. There's a lot more to pricing strategy once you hire or contract others. A lot of people I've seen were probably starting in the $20 an hour range but, again, you have to pay attention to the market. There are different rates in different regions. If you're in California, bookkeeping rates are going to be much more expensive than they are in Richmond, Virginia or in Wilmington, North Carolina. Don't set your prices just by what you read. Put some effort into pricing. Research and understand your market. Know what your competitors are charging. When I first started out, I knew what business owners were posting in their Craigslist ads for what they were looking for. I knew what CPAs were charging for bookkeeping work. I knew where I needed to be when I started. I didn't guess. It's important that you research your market and know what everybody else is charging.

A method I use to research competition and figure out what people are charging (without just going up to them and asking them), is by posing as a potential client. You can also get somebody else to pose as a client. Another method I used as I was growing and hiring people was to ask job candidates during our interview what they were charging clients at their previous employers. Many of them had worked at my competitors' companies. Don't miss out on the opportunity when you're talking to former employees of your competition to get as much intel as you can when you're interviewing them.

Don't just hide in a shell, a cocoon. You have to understand your industry. You need to understand what rates are being charged to make sure you're on top of it.

So, how did I decide to price for my services? Other than when I first came out of the gates with $15 an hour, as my business grew, I put a lot more thought into my pricing. It was usually based on the time I figured it was going to take and the complexity of the work I was going to do. And if a client comes to me with a tight deadline, I'm going to charge a little bit more because we're going to possibly have to work overtime to get that done. That definitely puts more value on the work we're doing if there's a tighter deadline.

PROPOSALS

As you do more proposals, you're going to get better at it. I put a lot of thought into my proposals. I never winged it or guessed at it. The bigger you get and the more infrastructure you tack on, the more overhead you tack on, you're definitely going to have to put more time and energy into how you price your services. When it's just you, you have a lot of flexibility. You can keep your overhead really low and figuring out what your price should be is fairly simple but, as you grow, it's going to get more complicated.

I typically would calculate some key metrics on each new job. For example, "What gross margin do I need to make?" factoring in what my fixed overhead was, and "How much gross margin do I need to make to target a specific net profit percentage?" A lot of people do it differently, but I started off with, "How much net profit do I want to make as a company?" and then I worked my way back up to what the gross margin should be. That ultimately led to the pricing decision.

You can't make the client pay for your uncontrolled overhead. Bookkeeping is a very competitive business. There are price pressures from overseas, price pressures from automated machines (AI), and small bookkeeping companies that don't have a lot of overhead. We always have pressures to keep our prices down. But at the same time, you can't keep raising prices. Make sure you build out a pricing model that factors in all your costs and delivers the gross profit you need to stay profitable. I would use an Excel spreadsheet and model out every job as part of my proposal process to make sure I had the right bill rate for that client. These pricing models will hold you accountable and allow you to adjust as your cost structure changes.

I had no problem talking to clients about pricing. I never guessed at it. I never wanted a client to question or think I was trying to take advantage of them, to think I was trying to gouge them. How did I know my pricing was good? As soon as my head hit the pillow at night, I fell asleep because I was not worried about whether I was taking advantage of somebody, that if anyone ever questioned me on how I came up with a price, I had no problem going over how I figured that price with them. And they knew that. So, I never really got a lot of pushback on my pricing.

That's all part of your *brand*, that's all part of your reputation. If you get a reputation as someone who gets as much money as they can, somebody that price gouges, somebody that can't back up their figures, you'll suffer for it. Clients are going to question you at every turn. They're going to question your invoices. They're going to question your timekeeping. I put enough effort upfront that I didn't get a lot of people questioning my prices, so I never really had to do much negotiation. I think that saves you a lot of time as well.

That doesn't mean I didn't negotiate. If I wanted to cut my fee a little bit, I would do that, but I could easily go to my calculations on the back end and see where I could save some money or do things differently.

I would encourage you to build a pricing spreadsheet that factors in all the things that are going to go into the job so you have a very good idea what your margin is going to be when you do that work. There's no tried or true reason on what your pricing should be. You have to figure that out based on all those factors. Ultimately, your pricing needs to be within the current market, and your pricing needs to be where you can make a profit.

HOURLY VERSUS FIXED PRICING

"How should I bill? Should I bill hourly or should I have a fixed monthly fee?" That is a common question asked within the accounting industry. Line up 10 people—half lean one way and half lean the other way. When I started my business, I started 100% hourly. Part of that was probably because I didn't know enough. Doing a monthly retainer back then wasn't as popular, but hourly *protected* me and it protected the client. And that's how I pitched it to clients. With an hourly agreement, it protects you as the service provider because you're going to make sure you get paid for all the time that you're working. For the client, their risk is mitigated because they're not going to pay for more than the time you worked.

There's nothing wrong with that method, especially when you're smaller, but as you grow and you start billing 40, 50, 60 clients, tracking those hours becomes quite an administrative burden. You also usually bill your hourly clients at the end of the month. For example, I work in the month of January, accumulate all those hours, and probably by the first week of February I produce an invoice for all the hours I worked in January. On the flip side, if I do a fixed or "retainer" fee, I charge at the beginning of the month for that upcoming month, and I create cash flow ahead of time. That is one of the advantages of billing on a fixed fee—you bill that typically at the beginning of the month versus an hourly fee, which you bill after the month is over.

At my company we used a mixture of both methods. Some clients just do not want to go with a fixed fee. I don't have a problem with that, but I certainly encourage using fixed or retainer fees. There's nothing to say you can't require a client to go on a fixed fee if that's the way you want to run your business. I always wanted to be flexible with my clients and give them as many opportunities to do business with me as possible.

The fixed fee pricing method requires you to be a lot more analytical. An hourly fee protects you. There's no risk that you're not going to get paid for hours you worked. With a fixed fee, there is that risk. If you estimate a job is going to take you 20 hours a month and at the end of the month you saw you put in 30 hours, well, you've already agreed to the 20-hour fixed fee. You will have to write off those 10 hours. A fixed fee definitely requires you to put in more thought to what your time involved is going to be.

When I quoted a fixed fee, I would usually say to the client, "Well, we've got to start somewhere. This isn't an exact science. This is my best guess based on what I'm seeing. We'll run with this for a few months. If it doesn't work, we'll sit down together and reprice it."

The first month of service is usually going to be estimated a little higher because it's a new client and you've got to learn the workflows, you've got to get all the logistics set up, and you're going to ask a lot more questions about their transactions. Don't panic if you go over budget in hours early on because things should settle down in a couple of months. You can't base a fixed fee off what that first month's going to look like, or you're going to overprice yourself.

The way I would sell a fixed fee to my clients is to explain, "It's a fixed fee, so you're not going to have any surprises. You're not going to get a huge bill in any particular month." It's easy for clients to budget a fixed fee. I would make sure to tell them, "Some months, I'm going to spend more time than what I budgeted. Some months I'm going to spend less time than I budgeted." So, as long as the workload and the fee even out over a period of six months (or whatever time frame you want to use), I didn't panic. I wouldn't run back to the client and say "Hey, I'm way over. I need to adjust my fee," because two months later you may be two or three hours under what you're billing them.

That doesn't mean you can't go back to the client and say, "Hey, I underestimated. The project is taking a lot more time than I thought," but you don't want to have a lot of those conversations. Hopefully, the more jobs you do and the more clients you work with, you get better at predicting your time.

I liked to make sure there was a consistent pattern of being over budget in hours before I went to the client and asked for any type of fee increase. Monitor your hours each month and set budgets for your bookkeepers. Let them know, "Hey, for this client I budgeted five hours a week." Your bookkeepers need to know it's five hours a week, and if they're consistently spending six or seven hours a week, you should be catching that if you're reviewing your timekeeping reports or your budget and job profitability reports. You want your bookkeepers to let you know, "Hey, I can't hit this budget," and find out where you missed it on the proposal. It's important you get that feedback from your bookkeepers, to make sure you're staying within the budget that you originally quoted on the contract.

Another fee arrangement option I use is where you agree to a fixed fee but add an hourly fee for anything over what the fixed fee covers. You're typically going to need preapproval from the client to do that, but that's a way to protect yourself if you go over your budget unexpectantly.

There's a lot of client management you'll need to do as you get bigger, and pricing, job profitability and budget versus actual analysis are important parts of that.

SET-UP FEES

One way to avoid losing money in that first month is to create a one-time setup fee. I sometimes charged new clients a flat $200 setup fee. That protected me and covered my time for setting up a QuickBooks file and chart of accounts, getting the banking logins, getting the banking ACH information to process their payments—basically getting their account set up in our system.

TIMEKEEPING

This leads us back to making sure you're doing proper timekeeping. There's nothing worse than spending a bunch of time on the clock and then trying to go back and figure out, "How much time did I spend on that client?" If you need to do the billing and you didn't track your time, there's a good chance you're going to overbill the client or underbill the client and you don't want to do that. As your company gets bigger your exposure increases as well. I suggest you use some kind of timekeeping system early on to track your hours. I suggest you do it every day. Don't wait until the end of the week or the end of the month, and then go back and recreate a time sheet.

There are plenty of timekeeping software packages out there that you could be using. And it's critical, particularly as you grow, that you know exactly the amount of time that you're spending on a client. When you're billing clients hourly, as long as you're keeping track of your time accurately, you have very little risk with that, which is what makes hourly pricing very attractive to a lot of bookkeepers and to a lot of clients as well. If you go to the fixed fee or the retainer fee, timekeeping becomes even more critical to you. It isn't as critical to your client because that fee is fixed. They don't care how much time you spend on their work because they know it's the same fee.

Again, don't panic if one month is a little bit higher or a little bit lower. Just watch the trend. And if you're consistently over budget on your time, then you need to go back to the client and have a very good explanation of why. Like I said, your bookkeeper can help you with that. For example, maybe the client added a couple of new accounts to the job since you first did the proposal, so that's going to have an impact on the hours worked.

SCOPE OF WORK

Part of your client contract which factors into your pricing is the *scope of work*. When I first started my company, I didn't really do any formal *scope of work* agreements with my clients. I just analyzed their business, saw how many credit cards they had, how many bank accounts they had, how many loans they had, what specific services they wanted me to perform, figured out how much time I thought that was going to take me, and there you go. But as I grew, I started to add specific scopes of work to all my contracts because you don't want to ever get into a battle with a client about whether a specific function is included in your agreement or not.

Fortunately, I haven't had to go back to that a lot. You try to communicate as best you can, but I definitely advise that whether you share that scope of work with your client and have it signed off as part of the contract, or it's simply noted internally within your own company, you should have a *scope of work* figured out. You should attach that to the budgeted hours that you give to the bookkeeper. For every job you're going to have a written proposal, you're going to have a contract agreement, and you should have a scope of work. Giving the scope of work to the client as part of the contract is a good idea, but at least you should have it for your internal bookkeepers, so they have a clear understanding of what the functions they're supposed to do are with each client, and what the anticipated time that it should take.

If a client contacts the bookkeeper and says, "Hey, I need help with this worker's comp audit," the bookkeeper should be able to pull up the scope of work and say, "Well, I don't see anything in here about a worker's comp audit. That's probably going to be an additional fee," or, "My scope of work is that we reconcile two credit cards for you. You've added two more since then. That's added time to the job. We're going to have to increase your fee."

The scope of work gives everybody a playbook, gets everybody on the same page, and allows the bookkeeper to have a reference to make sure the client is not consistently adding more work to the job and nobody's paying attention to it. If this happens, before you know it, your budgets are going to get way out of hand and the margins on those accounts are going to shrink and eventually go upside down. Having a scope of work is critical to your pricing and to making sure that your fixed monthly fee is always in real time. Again, if it's an hourly fee, it's not a big deal because you're just going to bill the client for how much work (i.e. hours) you're doing.

BLENDED RATES

Another potential pricing strategy is to come up with a *blended rate*. A *blended rate* is when you create separate pricing for each level of service you provide and then combine them into ONE billable rate. This pricing method is less likely if you are a sole proprietor and more likely if you have a staff and use more than one of them on a job. You might say, "I'm going to charge a lower rate for the entry-level bookkeeping functions like bank and credit card transaction imports and other basic tasks." That bookkeeper costs you less money, so the rate you would charge the client would be less. Then you might have a more senior-level bookkeeper on that same job, and that person does the bank reconciliations, reviews the general ledger, does more of the technical stuff, and that person bills out at a higher rate. So, you would charge that portion of the job at a higher rate. Then finally you might have a manager who oversees the job so you might factor in an hour of that person's time.

As you can see, you might have two or three different level people working on this one client's job. Instead of charging everybody out at one rate, that blended rate says, "These functions are at this rate and these functions are that rate." Add those up and you'll come up with a blended rate. This method requires a lot more thought and energy in a much more structured and detailed spreadsheet, but that's one way you can get more accurate in your pricing. It protects you from underpricing a job or overpricing a job.

As you build your business, you always want to delegate the work out as cost-effectively as you can. You don't want your highest-priced bookkeeper or accountant working on a client that you could be giving to an entry-level bookkeeper at a lower internal rate. There's a lot of management that needs to be done within your business in order to make your business more profitable.

PROFITABILITY

Internally assigning work so that you maximize the profitability on your clients ties into pricing because we can't let our pricing get out of control due to poor management of costs within our business. To remain competitive, you can't keep raising your fees every year. That's just not good business. If you start low, you can raise them over time, but at some point, you can't keep raising them because you're going to eventually price yourself out of that niche that you worked so hard to develop. And before you know it, you're competing in the same price category as the CPA firms, and that's not where you want to be.

Pay attention—don't let your costs drive your pricing so you're priced out of your market. Again, if it's just you, you should be able to handle that, but as you grow and get bigger, you have to continue to manage your costs so you can control your pricing.

NEGOTIATING PRICE

I put a lot of thought into my proposals, I always developed strong estimate worksheets. If you can think through everything and thus be able to justify every pricing decision, it gives you the confidence to walk away if the client doesn't like your price. I was open to negotiation, but I knew what my bottom line was. I knew I would never go below a certain price. As you grow and you build your brand and you build your business, you're going to be able to turn away a lot more business and be pickier with the clients you work with, so you'll get a lot more confidence in your pricing.

MINIMUMS

I didn't start using fixed fee *minimums* until just a few years ago. One of the challenges with my businesses (really *my* mindset) was that I wanted to help everybody I could. So, I probably took on more clients than I should have, but it was because I hated to turn anybody away. I hated to not help somebody because they weren't in a financial position to pay for it. I took on a lot of low-value clients, even up to a few years ago, just because of my mission and because I felt bad. Over time, I knew it was putting pressure on my staff to deal with so many clients. As a result, we were becoming less efficient.

Dealing with *lower value clients* takes you away from your *higher value clients*. You end up having to make a business decision at some point, regarding, "Do I set a minimum?" And we started to do just that. We kept minimums very low because I didn't want to price too many people out of the market, but you are going to have to price *some* people out of the market. You simply can't work with everybody (but remember, there is a solution out there for everybody). At some point, you're going to build your reputation as a professional services firm and people should pay for that. They should pay for your expertise. If they want a cheap low-cost provider, believe me, they're out there. Eventually, they will land on somebody who can service them.

That's the reality I had to come to grips with, that I couldn't help everybody, but that doesn't mean those people would not find help. I did implement some minimums and I think that helped manage our workload.

Cleanup versus Regular Work

As my business grew, I got more and more away from hourly work. When you have to go back and pull all the hours for all these jobs and then create invoices based off those hours, that's a lot of administrative work. So, I made the conscious decision to move more toward fixed-fee billing. All I have to do is create the invoice, memorize it in QuickBooks, and it posts automatically in my accounting system the first of every month. That allows you to service more clients with less administrative headaches.

The only hourly work I kept was *cleanup work*. I don't recommend you quote a fixed fee on cleanup work or project work, even though many business owners and clients will say that's what they want. They're going to tell you, "I need you to do this whole years' worth of work," for example, "How much is it going to cost?" Your first inclination might be that they're going to want a flat fee. Well, of course, they do. They want to protect themselves from paying a whole lot of money, but those are very hard jobs to quote a fixed fee for. After doing a couple of fixed fees, I realized you end up spending a lot more time than you thought you were going to on these cleanup jobs, so you typically don't make much money on them, if at all.

I decided any time a client came to me with several months' worth of work or more (clients have come to us with one or two years' worth of work), well, there's no way I can tell how much time that's going to take so I would tell them, "We'll do this cleanup/project work on an hourly basis. Then, after we're done, we recommend you become one of our month-to-month clients and we'll put you on a monthly retainer.

I would use that opportunity, as I was doing the cleanup work, to get a good understanding of the workflow for that client. By the time we got done with the cleanup work, I was very confident in how much time it would take once the books were clean to handle that client's work each month. The fixed fee actually became very easy to come up with. The client was happy because they could now budget how much their bookkeeping was going to cost each month.

I thought I would get a lot of pushback from clients on the hourly cleanup work approach, but we didn't. At the end of the day, you have to talk honestly and openly with your clients. I mean, these are other business owners, so I always say, "Just tell the truth!" Explain it in terms they would understand. Don't be afraid to talk openly and honestly with clients about your pricing. Talk to them about all the factors you took into account as you came to your decision, because the more they hear how much thought you put into it, the more they're going be receptive to accepting that price versus giving them a number out of the blue without any type of explanation. I always took time to let clients know how I came up with their prices.

With most of our cleanup work, we moved to 100% hourly billing. When clients come off the cleanup stage, we do a fixed monthly fee. I think you should charge more for cleanup work. If your hourly rate for a clean set of books is $40 an hour, I wouldn't charge $40 an hour for cleanup work. By definition, it's *cleanup*. It means you're going behind the work that somebody else did and they've butchered it pretty bad, it takes a lot more time and a lot more skill to fix what they messed up. We explain to the client, "This isn't just data entry. We have to go in and do journal entries. We have to fix what the other person did."

VALUE

In my opinion the bookkeeping industry is *devalued*. Part of the reason it's devalued is bookkeepers don't charge enough money for what they do. We are the gatekeepers of these businesses' cash and assets. A bad bookkeeper could potentially let a business go bankrupt. I am always astonished that people will pay a higher hourly rate to get a massage than they will pay their bookkeeper to manage their company's finances! Why would you go as cheap as possible to pay somebody to manage the highest value asset you have in your life? It doesn't make any sense to me.

I've always been a champion of charging what you're worth. That doesn't mean all business owners are going to accept your fees, but you should not be afraid to charge what you think you're worth. I was worth more than $15 an hour when I started, but I was starting and growing a business. I had to do what I had to do, but trust me, as my business grew, I absolutely charged what I thought my services were worth. And I got to the point where if a client didn't want to pay that fee, I said, "Thank you very much. Good luck to you."

Know your value. As bookkeepers, we need to fight for that value and promote our value and how important we are to the success of these businesses. I mean, think about it. We are providing financial information to business owners who are using that information to make very important business decisions. So, why not pay somebody good money to do that?

When you're doing your pricing, don't let business owners convince *you* what you're worth. Stick to your guns, *know* what you're worth, because you will find business owners who appreciate you. Don't be afraid to fire a client if the pricing structure doesn't work for you anymore. If you've got a client coming on and they're willing to pay you more money than another client is paying you, don't be afraid to either go back to that other client and ask them for a price increase or let them go because you need to focus your attention and your time on higher value clients.

Like anything, whether it's recruiting for clients, recruiting for employees or pricing, you never ever just sit back and let things happen to you. You have to be proactive. We preach to our clients *"know your numbers!"* Well, as bookkeepers you need to know YOUR numbers. You need to know what your market says your numbers should be. Be smart about your pricing. Don't just go off what you read in a pricing guide or what your friend told you or what somebody in Oklahoma told you what they charge for their bookkeeping services. That's certainly good to know but that doesn't mean that's how you should price your services.

You have to devote more time to thinking through what you should price each job. You should run a job profitability report on every job, in fact. You should be tracking your job profitability *throughout the lifecycle of that client*. Run reports and find out who your lowest margin clients are, and ask, "Is there an opportunity to raise my price? Has the scope of work changed?"

You need to constantly evaluate your jobs and make sure that the pricing is warranted, and don't be afraid to go ask for more money!

SUMMARY

Pricing is absolutely critical to the success of your business. If you model out each proposal based on what you think the cost structure is going to be, the pricing should be easy, but people get too emotional about it and they want to be liked. They don't want to lose a job. They don't want a messy conversation with the client. We don't like confrontation. In order to avoid confrontation, a lot of accountants might lowball or undersell their services because they don't want the pushback from the potential client. If you price everything low you're going to close a lot of business, but you're going to have a lot of business at very low margins and that's just not sustainable, particularly as you grow.

It's important you're confident in your estimates and you're confident in the way you present them to your clients. Often, the *way you present your pricing* to clients will dictate whether you get that client, or whether that client is going to give you any pushback. If you seem wishy-washy or the tone in your voice doesn't sound very confident, clients pick up on that. Just like in negotiation, people look for insecurity and weakness. If they see you're not 100% confident in your pricing, they're going to push back and probably beat you down to an even lower price. So, it's important you do the homework behind the scenes.

When you present a proposal to a client, and you know going in where your range is, if you do negotiate, you need to know what your *walkaway price* is. If you want to go in a little bit higher, that's fine, but know that you're not going below a certain point and you will turn away the business if they don't at least pay you that minimum.

It's important you put a lot of thought into your pricing. As you grow your business, you'll have a lot more pricing power. Something to look forward to!

CONTRACTS

I've always been a handshake kind of guy. I guess I'm old school. I believe in a handshake, but people mostly expect you to have a contract. I've been very fortunate in my 12 years of running Steiner Business Solutions. I recall just one time that I had to go back to a contract and that was actually for my tax business. On the bookkeeping side, I don't think I've ever had to go back to a contract to enforce anything, or sue anybody, and I've never been sued. My mindset is as long as you're happy and I'm happy, let's just keep working together, but the attorneys out there are going to fuss and say "Dan, you need to have a contract." So, I have contracts. I like to call them *agreements*. I think *contract* sounds too lawyerly. It sounds too confrontational to me. You're really just agreeing on terms to make sure we're all on the same page.

PREPARATION

Is it absolutely, critically, vital that you have proper contracts right out of the gate? No. You have very little risk when you're just dealing with a handful of clients. But as you grow, at some point when you feel you can invest in them, absolutely, set up the proper contracts. You can pay an attorney to draft an agreement for you, or to avoid an attorney, you might try LegalZoom or NOLO or some of the other online legal services out there to create a very basic agreement. Back in the day, when I first started, I paid an attorney. I think the contract was six pages long and they put *everything* in there. If you've ever worked with attorneys, you know they usually make contracts a lot more complicated than they need to be. So, over time I simplified it, whittled it down, adjusted it, modified it, to what I saw in the market as necessary. And today my agreement is *two* pages.

I don't want contracts to be what everybody focuses on. I tell clients, "I have to have this agreement (a) because my lawyer requires me to, and (b) it is a good reference point for us to revisit the basic terms." If there's a scope of work attached, it's a great opportunity to go back and see what the original scope of work was, but as discussed, it was quite a while before I started using scopes of work. Now I use them all the time. The bigger you get and the more clients you work with, the more exposure and risk you have so it's better to have a contract or an agreement in place to reference if and when you need it.

ACQUISITIONS

Another good reason to have agreements with all your clients is when you do go to sell your business, the buyer looking to acquire you will consider the agreements you have as part of their due diligence. They're going to want to see at least a copy of your current client contract. I can guarantee you they're going to ask, "Do you have written agreements, contracts with all your clients?" You might as well put the effort in early on to get those.

Still, I don't stress contracts with my clients. I don't want them to think we're starting our relationship with a legal mindset. I tell them, "This is just to confirm our basic terms. There's not a lot of crazy stuff in here. If you're ever unhappy with the work I do for you, then just tell me you're leaving. And that's it. I'm not going to hold you to anything. As long as you've paid up as far as we've worked for you, we're good."

TERMS

My agreements with clients are mostly month to month. I know not everybody does it that way. In fact, the general consensus in business *is* to get annual contracts whenever possible. An annual contract is much more appealing to a buyer of your business, but it was my decision early on not to go that route. I felt an annual contract created stress on the proposal and I didn't want to create a barrier to entry. Fortunately it worked out well for me having my clients on month-to-month agreements. If you've built a great brand, and you have loyal clients who have been with you for years, who needs a contract? When potential buyers came to evaluate my business, I told them, "I have to be honest, I don't have agreements on hardly any clients from early on. I only started using them regularly within the last few years." The buyers were okay with that, but only because they knew my reputation. They looked at how long my clients had been with me, and concluded my clients weren't going anywhere, at least not for lack of a contract.

I can't think of a reason to *not* have a contract with a client. But in my opinion, you don't want to lead off with a lot of legalese when you're talking with small business owners because they're usually intimidated by a lot of legalese. I still tell them, "It's more of our onboarding paperwork. It's just a reference point for us to keep in your file we can always go back to if needed." Downplay it to a point.

Some might say, "No, I'd rather lock them in for six months or for a year," and if you can do that, that's great. When you're starting out and you're just trying to sign up clients, I don't know that I would lead off with "Sign this annual contract" with somebody you've never met before. My advice is to not come out of the gate with annual contracts or even a specific-term contract. Instead, start off with a month-to-month agreement, and build your reputation. Clients want to know if it doesn't work out or they're not happy or they feel like they got a bad bill of goods they have an exit option.

SCOPE

It's important to add that I put in all of my agreements, "If further work is required outside of the original scope, Steiner Business Solutions will provide a separate agreement for that service before the service is provided." It has protected me from clients who tried to dump more work into our original agreement.

INVOICING TERMS AND PENALTIES

When we talk about invoicing, we talk about *when* to invoice— once a month? twice a month? on the first of the month? mid-month? And we talk about payment terms. Are your invoices due on receipt, or are they due within 30 days? And is there a late fee or an interest charge if the balance goes unpaid after 30 days?

You want to set the tone right away that you're not going to put up with late payments. One of the key sentences I put in all my agreements in the invoicing section is the very last sentence that says, "Services may be interrupted by an overdue account." Mitigate your risk. If a client is not paying you, figure out your threshold for pain. Mine was that I rarely ever went more than 60 days working without a payment. If a client was 30 days past due, I started getting on them, but if it got to be 60 days past due, I would simply contact the client or the bookkeeper would contact the client and say, "Look, we're going to have to stop working on your account until you get your account caught up because I can't keep going on paying my people to work on an account where we're not getting paid."

I limited my exposure. After 60 days, I stopped doing the work. If you're doing payroll for a client, that's a great way to put a shock in their system and say, "Well, look, your people aren't going to get paid next week unless you get your account with us caught up." That usually got their attention and usually got a payment from them.

Be very descriptive in that invoicing section about when payments are due and what happens if they don't pay on time.

DISCLAIMERS

Other verbiage I include in our contracts reads, "Steiner employees or contractors working on your account are not considered employees of your company." It means we want to discourage *my* employees going to work for my clients. I also include, "You cannot solicit my employees or contractors to come work for you. If you do or you want to talk to me about hiring one of my employees, there would be financial compensation."

It's important to protect yourself from clients poaching your employees and/or contractors. These bookkeepers are working hand-in-hand with clients. Clients develop a relationship with my bookkeepers. They rely on the bookkeepers heavily and it's very common that the clients are going to want to not pay your company for that employee. They think they might get your employee to work for them at a lower rate. So, you want to protect yourself with a clause in your agreement.

TERMINATION

While I do include a *termination clause* in our agreements, I never focused much on this. This was more for the client. A client always likes to have that exit option. I used a 30-day term in agreements, very standard stuff. I told clients, "Look, I would love to get 30 days' notice but, at the end of the day, if you're not happy and you don't think we're doing right by you, you can leave anytime. I'm not going to hold you to a specific term."

If, however, as your business grows and you accumulate larger, high-value clients, you'll be putting a lot of resources into that one client and a 30-day notice just isn't enough time. I've had some of my higher-end clients on a 60-day notice term because if you're losing that big chunk of revenue, you want to have more time to figure things out on your back end to pivot.

If and when termination does occur, I think it's important you *do not release* any of their documents, financial data, QuickBooks files, or other account information of theirs until their account is fully paid and in good standing. This is something you learn over time and with experience. We used to hand everything over to be *good guys,* only to find their account was in some cases 60 days behind.

CONFIDENTIALITY

An important item for clients is that their information is not going to get into the wrong hands, that you're going to keep good track of it, that you're not going to give it to third parties. I have a pretty big confidentiality clause in all my agreements. Much of it is legalese, but just seeing there is a commitment to confidentiality on my company's part is great comfort to most clients.

OTHER CLAUSES

There are certainly other clauses that can be included in contracts, many specific to you and your business. We've had *server access* clauses, for example. If we host their QuickBooks file on our server, we have something in there about the rules of access to our server. When we provide bill payment services for clients, we include a bill payment clause that addresses access to their banking accounts and signature requirements. In general, it's good to start with a lot more than you need and then kind of whittle it down as things change or evolve. Cyber security is a big thing, for example, so you might want to put a clause in there about what your company does regarding cyber security. You might put something in about backing up data. The point is your contracts and agreements need to change with the times. Don't just build a template and fill in the blanks. I never do that. Certainly, you want to have a template to start with, but rarely are any two contracts the same.

Before I obtain signatures on an agreement, I read that agreement word-for-word, every time. Even though I know it's the same agreement I use for all my clients, I still read it. I still make sure I didn't put something in there I will regret later because it was something that I used for another client. Definitely read your agreements before you execute them. From time to time it's a good idea to have an attorney look it over, along with any of your peers or business partners.

INDEPENDENT CONTRACTORS

More than likely before you hire an employee, you're going to bring on an independent contractor. If you hire someone to help you with bookkeeping, you absolutely need to have a written agreement with that person. You're now getting into more risk, dealing with someone to pay, dealing with their livelihood, and you've exposed your client(s) to another person other than yourself. You have someone with access to documents, technology, computers, and client files. You have an "outsider" with access to personal and confidential information. It's vital that you do have an agreement or a contract with any independent contractor that you bring into your business.

I've had them from the beginning and I haven't made a lot of changes. I'm willing to pay to get it done right so I had an attorney draft my independent contractor agreement.

If your contractor is only going to work on one client, then you should put the client name and those specific services they're going to do for that client in the agreement. As you grow and a contractor might be working on multiple clients, you might state that "the bookkeeper is going to provide general bookkeeping services," for example. But I don't recommend you do one contractor agreement for every single client that contractor works on. I would probably do one overall general contractor agreement and then have an addendum that you keep adding client names to, with specific pay rates.

If you're going to have the same pay rate for every client that contractor ever works for, then you could put the contractor pay rate on the main agreement. You need to be very clear about what the contractor is going to pay for versus what you're going to pay for. By definition, for people to be properly classified as independent contractors, they should be supplying a lot of their own equipment and supplies. If there's something they're buying specifically on your behalf, you need to have some kind of reimbursement policy clearly stated.

You need to be very clear in your contracts that this person *is* a *contractor*. There is a lot of regulation on what a *contractor* is, versus an *employee*. There are heavy fines and penalties if you're misclassifying people who work for you. So, you want to be very clear in your agreements with your contractors that they're not employees. They are independent contractors. I have in my agreements that if they stop working for me, they have to return any and all equipment and client paperwork—anything I provided to them to perform their duties, they have to return back to me.

I put a lot in their contract about confidentiality. They can't divulge information about my clients, and they also can't divulge information about my business practices. They have to keep the details of our working relationship confidential.

Another clause I use concerns non-solicitation of customers. That's huge. You have to have that in your agreements that you don't want independent contractors out there stealing your clients. If you think about it, if you get an independent contractor and you give them six or seven clients, guess what, they might say, "Hey, I can start my own business. I got six or seven clients now who love me. All I have to do is tell them I'm starting my own bookkeeping business. Why don't you just come over to my company? I'll give you a better rate."

That's why I say you need to have something in your client agreements that protect you from that situation, but you also need to have some of that language in your contractor agreements to protect you from that situation because the bigger you get and the more contractors you use, there's a good chance your clients are going to get poached by these contractors. Fortunately, I didn't run into a big problem with that. I think part of it is you set the tone when you hire that if they're caught trying to steal clients or poach clients, you're going to terminate them, and remind them they signed an agreement that says they are not allowed to solicit clients. So, it's important you have a clause in your agreements that discourages and penalizes contractors if they try to start their own business by stealing clients from you.

There can be a lot of *legalese* in a contractor agreement because, again, these people are representing you to your clients, they're representing you in the community. I definitely wouldn't craft such an agreement on my own. I would get your attorney to craft your contractor agreements.

SUMMARY

I paid good money to have my contracts done. It's worth it, because one of the key things you want to do is protect yourself and your company. It's important you have good contracts because the more infrastructure you have in your business, the more *valuable* your business will be to an outsider. A buyer wants to be able to come into a business and know there is very little risk, that you have locked in your processes, your procedures, that you have contracts and agreements, and they are not coming into a risky situation.

[5] RISK – BE HONEST!

IT'S IMPORTANT that anyone who decides they want to start a business or continue being in business, recognize there's a level of risk in doing so, and that everyone self-evaluate what level of risk they're comfortable with. I don't think anyone is born with a certain level of risk tolerance and that's all you're destined to have. I think as you build up more confidence in yourself and in your knowledge of your business, there's a tendency for you to take more risks.

I came up just like every other accountant and there's a tendency for us to be taught to avoid too much risk. It's particularly the stereotype of accountants and CPAs, that we're averse to risk, that we don't take chances, that we like things to go in sequence—1-2-3-4, A-B-C-D. By and large, that's very true. I'm an accountant by trade but I developed into an entrepreneur with a whole different mindset about risk, and I think it's paid off for me up to this point. Anyone interested in starting a business or currently running a business constantly needs to determine what they're willing to take on in terms of risk. To help with that, we should talk about how to mitigate your risk.

EXAMPLES

Everything you do in life has some form of risk. Particularly in a business, every decision you make has a cost-benefit relationship to it. For example:

- You're taking a risk when you decide to charge a client a new higher fee.
- You're taking a risk every time you put out a new proposal.
- Hiring a new contractor or employee is very risky! We're going to get into that in the next chapter. Your *first* employee is going to be the toughest one, but believe me, every employee after that is risky as well.
- Firing a client is risky.
- Firing employees has risk, and that's a very tough decision for any business owner. It could be a financial decision, or it could be philosophical—maybe this person's just a bad apple with a bad attitude. It could be work ethic. It could be any number of reasons you need to fire an employee, but that's a risky decision. Who's going to do the work when that person leaves? If you terminate that employee, have you exposed yourself to any legal issues?
- You're taking a risk just by starting a business. You're giving up that steady paycheck. You usually don't know how long you're going to go before you can take a

paycheck. You're sacrificing family time. So, there's a lot of personal risk that you take on.

- And then we get into debt. I have a lot of conversations with business owners about debt. A lot of people want to get into a business without getting into too much debt because debt is risky (and scary). That's true, but when most of us buy a house, we get a mortgage on that house. Well, that's risk. If you can't pay the mortgage, you could lose your house. I use that analogy with business owners with their businesses and say "Well, look, this (your business) potentially could be your largest asset, worth even more than your home. Why wouldn't you use debt to help it grow, to maintain it, to improve it? What's the difference?" Sometimes the light bulb goes off when I use that analogy because it's true.

When you start a business, everybody bootstraps and tries to spend as little money as possible. And I agree with that. You should go in with a controlled budget, but at some point, if you are going to grow, if you are going to expand, you're going to need to take on some form of debt. There are lots of different ways to do that. The quickest and easiest one for most people is to use credit cards.

I encourage you to get a corporate credit card with the same bank you have your operating account with. Don't be lazy and use your personal credit cards for business purchases. I'm sure I don't have to tell you that! Get that corporate card. It will help build your credit relationship with your bank and you want strong relationships with your banks. The banks are the folks who are hopefully going to help you grow along the way.

LINES OF CREDIT

I always encourage small business owners to get a line of credit. Typically, with banks these days, you're going to need to be in business at least a couple of years for them to even talk to you about a line of credit.

They're very convenient to use and you only pay interest if you draw on the line of credit. I would use it as your safety net, in case something happens, the economy goes bad, you lose an employee, or if you lose a bunch of clients, you'll have that line of credit to fall on. I know with my business, I'd ask for as much money as I could get, based on my financial situation at that time. Typically these lines renew every year or two and every time the renewal came up, I'd resend them my financial statements and tax returns and I'd ask, "Now how much can I get?" If I had a $10,000 line before and could now get $25,000, I went to $25,000.

That didn't mean I immediately spent $25,000, but I liked to get as much credit available to me at all times. Again, you're not paying any interest on that money until you draw on it. So, if you have a $25,000 line but you only draw $5,000 off of it to use, you're only going to pay interest on $5,000. I encourage you to continue to increase your line of credit amount each renewal period (if capable) to have as much cash available to use for your operations. I used my lines of credit for capital improvements and big expenditures, but also for potential acquisitions. If there was a small acquisition out there and I needed to put my hands on some cash for a down payment, I used my lines of credit. And if the line of credit interest was cheaper than my credit card interest, I would use my line of credit.

Those are the typical "low risk" debt instruments I recommend for small businesses to use routinely. It's risky to take on debt but, again, with a line of credit, that debt is only there if you use it, and a line of credit actually *mitigates your overall business risk.*

That's what this chapter is about—how do we evaluate risk, how do we take advantage of it, but also mitigate any potential losses that may come around? A line of credit is a good way to mitigate your risk. If something did happen to you, if you did have to fire some clients, if you did have to fire an employee, if the economy did go sideways, your line of credit is there to help fill that cash void.

STREAMS OF REVENUE

Another good way to mitigate your risk is to add new revenue streams. If your bread and butter is bookkeeping, you've got to try to figure out other ways you can bring additional revenue into your business. For me, I created a QuickBooks training division; I created a tax company; and I figured out other ways that I could bring in revenue, just in case. Go back to your existing clients and ask them if there is any additional work you could do for them, any other projects they could use help with. They often don't really know what you can do, even if you say it on your website or other marketing materials.

It's important you communicate with your clients. They're on the front lines. They're the ones in the trenches. They're not thinking about you every day, believe it or not. In fact, you're probably one of the last people they think about. So, it's important for you to stay in touch with them and find out what sort of challenges and issues they're facing and if there is any potential opportunity for you to help them with that. That's potentially going to create new revenue streams for you, and that will protect you. It will also look very good in your client's eyes that you're being proactive. I encourage you to constantly reach out to your clients to find other opportunities for you to help them.

SELF-HONESTY

A dilemma we all face as business owners is whether to stay small or to go big. Trust me, it's okay if you change your mind a few times. I've done it plenty of times! It's okay if you want to stay small, but for those who want to go big, it means you're going to have to take bigger risks, you're going to have to have a higher tolerance for failure, you're going to have to have a higher tolerance for stress. Believe me, the bigger you get, the more employees you have, the more HR issues you have to deal with. You've heard the term, *More Money, More Problems?* It's true.

I went back and forth on whether to stay small or go big when I first started Steiner Business Solutions. My early vision was to have offices all over the United States, whether that was a franchise system or a licensed system. All my employees would wear the same polo shirts and khaki pants, and they would show up at people's offices and provide bookkeeping services for them. I had this big dream! Of course, I had a business plan written. I talked to a local CPA about opening up another Steiner Business Solutions office in town, and that just never panned out. We tried to expand that way for about a year and it just didn't work.

Instead of knocking my head against the wall, I pivoted and moved on and decided the best way for me to grow was through acquisitions. It's very hard to open up new offices in other markets organically. It's easier to do it through acquisition. So that's what I did. I grew my business through acquisitions. I went from three or four employees one year, to having 17 employees the next year, and then I was up to over

25 employees within another year! But when I got to that point, I started getting more and more frustrated. I was spending more time putting out "fires" instead of working with my clients – doing the work I love. The fun started to go away and after much reflection, I decided that was as big as I wanted to get.

As it turned out, I ended up selling my bookkeeping division because I knew that just wasn't the revenue model I wanted to pursue. I went from wanting to have thousands of employees all over the country, to just having me and a couple others—just a few of us to manage and oversee the business, which was much more my style. It allowed me to do things I enjoyed, which was the advisory and mentoring services. I had changed my mind several times and that's okay. You're going to change your mind from time to time, and you should. You don't want to get stuck in your ways and try to force yourself into a particular size, force yourself into a partnership or a relationship with somebody who you probably shouldn't have gotten into business with. It's important that you're just honest with yourself.

Don't beat yourself up if you have to change your mind or pivot. You're not going to have all the answers. You must be willing to change but you can't drag your feet. That's very important. *Indecision* is very risky, and it gets down to those examples I pointed out earlier. You don't want to wait too long to fire a bad employee, you don't want to wait too long before firing a bad client, and you don't want to wait too long before increasing a fee. If you wait too long, that's costing you money.

If you were so nervous about raising your fees, either with one client or across the board, the profitability on your jobs is going to suffer and that's going to eat away at your profits over time. It could have a pretty big impact. A bad employee can cause irreparable damage to a business. Indecision is one of the worst things you can do when you're evaluating risk. The key is *spending the time*. If you have to get away from the office, if you have to go outside and just think on it, if you have to get out of the day-to-day bustle, spend that time to evaluate key decisions. And make them.

Be honest with yourself and ask for help. Talk to somebody. I run a monthly peer group and I've had several business owners in that peer group whom we challenged to reach higher. At the beginning of the year, we write out our goals for what we want to accomplish in the upcoming year. More often than not the group will push each member to reach even higher with their goals. The *risk* is that you're going to set the bar too low. My goal with this book is to *tell* you and *show* you that you can, if you risk more, achieve more! And if you fail to reach your goal, it doesn't wipe you out completely.

You have to make sure you've got protections in place so if you do take a risk and it doesn't work out, it doesn't totally put you out of business. It's very important you figure out your *breakeven point*. What's the number, metric, or the event that determines you will scale back, push the pause button, walk away? You have to determine that. You can't go blindly into opportunities, blindly into risks you take. You have to have a kill switch which says, "This is as far as I'll go," and hit it when an opportunity doesn't seem to be working out *because another opportunity will come along*, and you've got to be ready for it.

YOUR NUMBERS

We tell our clients all the time they need to *know their numbers*. How can you make a good, informed decision, how can you evaluate risk properly, if you don't know your numbers? It's important. For one thing, you've got to have a solid timekeeping system. There are plenty of software applications for this—T-Sheets is one that I've used in my business and I recommend to a lot of my clients. You have to keep track of your time and if you have employees, you have to track their time. If you bill hourly, how do you know you're billing the right amount to clients? And if you bill on retainer, it's very easy to set the fee and then leave it alone. If you charge $600 a month and you're not paying attention to the hours that are going into the job, that's *risky*. Things change. So, keeping time is just a perfect example of knowing your numbers.

How can you evaluate whether a client is good or bad for you and your business if you can't run a legitimate profitability report on those clients? You've got to know your numbers. You've got to stay involved with *all* aspects of your business. Don't get carried away with sales. I see lots of business owners spend all their time networking and chasing revenue and that's great, you need to bring in business, but you also need to understand if you are making money.

DEBT

As discussed earlier in this chapter, in order to grow, you're going to need to use some form of debt. In all likelihood you're going to deal mostly with banks. You might also deal with investors, and maybe friends that are going to loan you money as well, but in any case, you have got to understand what outsiders are looking for in your business. How do they evaluate your business for risk? You need to know that because you need to build your business so that it looks less risky from the outside. *What kind of debt-to-equity ratio are they looking for?* When someone's going to lend you money, they want to first know if you are able and likely to service the debt. *Can you make your monthly payments? Does your business generate enough cash every month to pay the monthly payments?*

Meet with your bankers. It's important to establish relationships with them. Your network of friends and business contacts are vital to you. They are a great risk mitigator. I lean on my network all the time. If a new piece of legislation comes out and I'm not comfortable understanding what it's saying, I'm going to contact my business attorney and get their perspective on what that legislation means and what it means to my business.

And lean on your bankers. It's important that bankers understand you—not just your business—because everything in business is about relationships. The joke is bankers only want to lend you money when you don't need it, and there's a lot of truth to that, but you need to invest the time for them to understand your business and to build trust because you never know when you're going to need them. I have great relationships with several banks. It's great to be able to pick up the phone and tell them, "I need something." And I typically don't go through as much red tape to get a resolution, which saves me a lot of time and energy. Sometimes they're open to waiving or lowering some of the fees—process fees, document fees, whatever they might charge on a loan—because I'm a good client and they've got a great relationship with me.

If you go to a bank and they turn you down, you need to understand why they turned you down. Ask, "What do I need to do to resubmit this loan so that it *can* get approved?"

"Well," they might say, "you need to have another $10,000 of cash showing in your checking account," or, "You've got this credit card. The balance is too high. You've got to get that balance down under a certain amount of money."

Then go pay the credit card balance down as opposed to moping around saying, "I got turned down from this bank. I can't believe they did that. What am I going to do? Okay, I'll try another bank." That's not the right approach. Always negotiate. Always work the system. It's easy just to say no and walk away but that's not the approach I recommend. Fight with these banks and fight with these other vendors to get them to work with you. That's very important.

Always be forward thinking. Be prepared. That's actually what I'm saying when I say, "Know your numbers." I realize these things take time. I mean, just to do an SBA loan could take months. A line of credit might take 30, 45, maybe 60 days to secure. When you start getting into traditional loans through banks, particularly with the SBA, it's usually going to take a good amount of time, maybe months, before that loan closes and you get your money. That's another reason to consider a line of credit because if you need a *fast* infusion of cash, a traditional loan is not going to do that. I would rely on lines of credit for anything you need in the near term.

So, we have to be forward thinking. We have to plan ahead. These should be tips and advice you're giving to your small business clients. All business owners need to think of the future. If your growth goals are XYZ, you've got to map out how you're going to get there. There are going to be risks along the way:

- You're going to have to hire employees,
- You might have to lease office space,
- You might have to take on debt.

You just don't go from point A to point B without there being quite a bit of decision-making along the way. That requires proper planning and you want to be truthful with yourself on how much time that's going to take—not just *calendar* time but *your* time. Do you have the capacity, the bandwidth? Does your staff have the bandwidth to take on these challenges down the road? It's risk-reward, it's cost-benefit analysis that you need to be working on.

SUMMARY

Every decision you make, everything you do, everything you *don't do,* is risky. Indecisiveness and inaction are often just as risky as taking action. I read a lot of business books and there's a lot of great advice out there. My goal with *this* book is to give you hope that there IS opportunity, that if you DO take risks and you take them intelligently, you will be rewarded and there is a pot of gold at the end.

I watch and listen to other business owners and I can get pretty frustrated because they complain about this or they complain about that, and I always say, "Well, what are you doing about it?"

They'll give me excuses and explain why they can't do it. "I'm nervous," they might say. "I don't know if this is going to work."

And I say, "Well, how are you going to know if it's going to work if you don't try?"

If you want to grow and you want to scale and you want to have a liquidity event when you decide to retire and sell your business, the owners who took the risks, took the chances, and identified the opportunities, are the ones who are going to benefit the most from taking those actions. If you don't want to take a lot of risks, if you don't want to take a lot of chances, if you don't want to get out into your community, if you don't want to read up on what's going on in your market place, if you just want to sit at home or sit at your office and do bank reconciliations, you could have a very good job but you're not going to make a lot of money and you're not going to retire wealthy. There's nothing wrong with that, but this book is really, hopefully, for those who want to achieve *wealth* with their business.

Accountants, by nature, are risk averse. That's probably why in our industry there aren't many bookkeeping businesses who scale to any significant size, and there probably aren't many bookkeepers who are creating wealth with their business. They just kind of treat it as a job. They're not sure how to face or how to deal with the challenges that are going to confront them. They're very conservative in nature.

Believe me, through my career, I've put everything at risk, but my spouse and my family have supported me through all of it. The most successful people, the most successful business owners, the most successful athletes, you name it, were the ones who were willing to risk everything, the ones that were willing to risk losing their house, willing to risk family time. Those are the ones who were able to acquire wealth and have that exit, that sale, that liquidity event when they sold their business.

Hopefully this book will resonate with you and change your mindset. Losing clients is not a bad thing. Firing employees is not a bad thing. It just creates a new opportunity. *When one door closes, another one opens.*

There have been plenty of setbacks along the way for me. I've had several failed businesses but that didn't stop me. I've started and/or partnered in eight or nine different businesses by now, many of them not even related to the accounting industry. Obviously, failure did not stop me from trying the next one. All those times I failed, I made sure it did not impact my main business, Steiner Business Solutions, because that was always going to be my bread and butter. That was the business that was going to provide my exit strategy. Most of my other businesses ventures were in other industries you don't see accountants getting into very much. Those were more to satisfy my need for new challenges. I also *learned* a lot from running those businesses. Those experiences have made me a better business owner and a better consultant to my clients.

This book highlights how I aggressively went after my dream and became successful creating wealth. I did it and YOU CAN TOO!

[6] WHEN AND HOW TO HIRE

THIS IS THE *WALL* (as I call it) that most business owners hit at some point which holds them back from really growing—*when to hire that first person.* It seems like there should be an easy answer, right? You hire someone when you run out of capacity to do more work, right? When you start your business, you're usually the *sole* proprietor. I started my business at a very low hourly rate, but I knew going in that for me to grow, I was going to have to bring on higher paying clients. Well, if you bring in new clients at a higher rate, you're going to have to go back to your original clients and raise their rates to your new rate, or you're going to lose those clients. There's really no other way, if you're going to stay by yourself, to handle that. So many people *stay small.*

This book is not for those people. This book is for people who do want to grow and scale their business.

CONTRACTORS

When I started, I did all the work I possibly could. I didn't work 9 to 5. Instead, I filled up my workload as much as I could. I probably worked from 8 in the morning till 11 o'clock at night five days a week, and I worked many weekends. I worked as much as I possibly could until I couldn't do any more or it got in the way of other things. But when you're a business owner, you can't just do client work. You also have to handle your insurance, your marketing, your social media, you have to attend meetings, you have to network, do proposals, and there's admin time you have to carve out as any business owner does.

When I consult with people, I tell them "everybody is a profit and loss statement." When you're a sole proprietor, you have a lot more control over the money you bring in and the money you spend. When you bring in revenue, you get to keep all that revenue for yourself outside of paying your overhead expenses. It's a much different ballgame when you bring in other people, when you hire. *You have to be profitable as a sole proprietor before you can even consider bringing in an employee.* You're going to have to hire another employee once you have met certain conditions:

A) You're profitable
B) You can't take on any more work
C) You want to grow and scale

As I brought on new clients and my workload was growing, I could be a little picky about the next client I brought in. It's important you figure out what your *cost of labor* is going to be when you're ready to hand off work to a contractor or employee. I remember when I signed up my first *big client* early on, which was a home healthcare agency. I billed them $30 an hour and I thought that was the best thing ever. Not only was the rate *twice* as much as I was charging when I first started, but there were quite a lot of hours involved.

I knew for me to take on this new client, I was going to have to offload some of my existing (cheaper) work. In order to stay profitable, I had to find somebody who would do it for less $15 an hour. That was a profit and loss decision. If you're in a crunch and you've got to get started on that $30 an hour client immediately, you might bring somebody in for $15 and understand that even though it's a breakeven situation on that client, it's still in your best interest. You don't want to lose the client. You are better off breaking even on that client than losing the client altogether. Down the road you can raise that client's fee to get yourself profitable.

While I was doing all the work myself and I couldn't do much else, that didn't stop me from looking for new clients. I was looking to grow. So, I found this new client, a higher paying client, and I didn't have the capacity to work all the hours that were required. I decided to hire somebody and offload some of my work. I'm not going to offload all of my work, at least not at this stage, but I have to offload at least some of this work. Since I'm offloading just a partial amount, I probably have to go look for a contractor rather than an employee. An independent contractor is typically not going to be looking for full-time work. They're going to have their own capacity issues. I evaluate and ask the contractor, "What's your capacity and availability?" If they tell me, "I've got 10 hours a week available," I'll say "Great." I then go through my list of clients and find out if I have 10 hours a week to give this person. If that means there are two clients who get that person nine hours a week, that's great. I'm then going to take two clients off of me and give them to the contractor and, hopefully, that's going to free up enough time for me to service this new client. If it's not enough time, then I'm going to have to go find another contractor. Then it gets into the management of figuring out each contractor's capacity.

I went quite a while before I hired my first full-time employee. Using independent contractors is a great way to grow your business without having to commit to a certain salary or to a certain number of hours. Contractors are much more flexible to do piecemeal work than a full-time employee is. Therefore, I recommend you start off with independent contractors. As the work starts to pick up you've got to recruit. Before now, you were only recruiting for new clients. Now you're at a stage where you've got to find *contractors*. Contractors come in all shapes, forms, and sizes. I used to have contractors who didn't want to work certain days of the week, some couldn't work certain hours of the week, some didn't want to go to certain parts of the city. So, you really have to spend a lot of time building a database of independent contractors.

You've got to understand what each contractor's limitations are as far as being able to do the work. I had a stable of four or five contractors at any given time because when a new job comes in, you've got to match it up to the right contractor. That's a lot of work. Contractors come and go, so you are going to have to spend a lot of your time over the course of your business looking for contractors. At some point you're going to be looking for employees as well. That's how I started to offload my work. I wanted to stay relatively busy, but I never wanted to be at full capacity, personally, because I always knew I had other things to do to as the owner, to *run* my business. I always got up to a certain point in billable time—maybe 60% or 70%, and I left the other 30% to do the networking, the business development, marketing, and things like that, but I always also tried to accommodate my contractor's wishes.

I always want contractors to work with me exclusively. I didn't like the idea of potentially losing a contractor to another firm. If a contractor came to me and told me they had 15 hours a week of capacity, I did everything I could to get them to the 15 hours. It might mean I had to give them an additional client, off my workload, but I knew by that point I could get more work in the door. In fact, it motivated me to get more work because I knew I had some available capacity. But ultimately, my priority was always to get my contractors up to *their* capacity. When they were at full capacity, I knew I had to go find another contractor. Then I would try to get that contractor up to their capacity and keep them happy so they stay in the system. It's hard to find good people, so I did everything I could to keep them happy. If I had to sacrifice some of my own billable time, that was okay.

You have to find different levels of contractors. Some of them will have more expertise in QuickBooks than others. Some of them have specific industry experience that you might want. Some of them are going to ask for a different labor rate than others. You've got to make sure each contractor (and every employee) has their own *profit and loss statement*. If you're not making money on the work you're giving to them, you're doing something wrong. If you know you have to strategically price your jobs to account for whatever the cost of labor is on that job, it's very simple. *Gross profit is going to be sales less cost of sales, and your cost of sales is the labor.* So, if you want to make a 60% gross margin, then you've got to price your services at a high enough fee that gives you 60% gross profit *after* you pay your contractor.

It's important, if you want to stay profitable, that you are paying attention to the P&L of each of the contractors you bring in. That's how I grew. I would hand off my work to a contractor, get them full, leave myself exposed, and that just motivated me to get more work. I always had a lot of confidence I would get the work, that was never an issue for me, and I hope that's not going to be an issue for you if you follow my suggestions and advice on how to get clients. You're always going to have confidence that more work is going to come in and you're going to bring in higher-priced work, and that was usually the strategy I had. I would personally do the higher-value work, the more complicated and technical jobs. I would not give work to a contractor if I didn't think they were capable of doing it. I didn't want to hurt my brand by delegating the more complicated work. And I was able to price work right way, knowing what my cost of labor was.

You should recruit contractors *before* you even have a ton of work to give them because you need to know what those labor rates will be. I've talked consistently about learning your market. You've got to know what the competition is paying people in your business, whether they're contractors or employees. You've got to be able to match up the labor rate with that person's skill level. You have to have the confidence and the ability to evaluate whether that person is worth what they state as their rate because you're going to have to price that work to the client, and you have to justify to the client that the level or complexity of work requires that kind of retail price.

At the same time, you can't let your contractors dictate what your retail price is going to be. They are going to factor into it, but if it's entry level work and you know you can't charge more than $40 an hour to the client, well, you don't then want to pay a contractor $30 an hour to do that work. That doesn't give you enough margin. Honestly, the market for that work likely wouldn't pay somebody $30 an hour. Tt's important you don't blindly sign up contractors. Their labor rates are going to influence your retail rates and you will start getting pushback, losing work, because your retail rates are too high for the type of work you're doing.

Make sure you're hiring contractors at all pay levels, all skill levels, and make sure you match up the work to the right person. You don't want to have 15 different retail rates to customers. I typically had a price range for services. I charged a higher rate for cleanup work, but if it was entry-level, basic work, we didn't charge more than $50 an hour. In your pricing you always have to evaluate the complexity of the work and what is it going to cost you to find somebody to do that work. That is going to play into what your retail rate is, and you have to pay attention to both sides of the equation. You have to understand what the market is paying people to do that work. Then you have to find out what accounting firms are charging small business owners for that work. You can't be too high or too low in either one of those categories. You have to pay attention to both of them if you want to be successful and remain highly profitable.

EMPLOYEES

When do you hire an *employee*? That's a tough question because there are more costs that come with employees. You typically don't have enough work to fill up an employee's time if they're looking for 40 hours per week. I wasn't sitting on 40 hours of available work not already being done by somebody. I was usually at capacity and my contractors were at capacity. This is where the risk-reward comes into play. Typically, this is what my thought process looked like when I was evaluating the need to hire a full-time bookkeeper:

I'd first look at the number of clients I had with contractors. I would look at the amount of work I had, and I'd figure out, *If I took all the client work off these two contractors and gave it to my new employee, how much billable time does that give the employee?* Maybe I could give them 15 or 20 hours a week from my contractors. And then I'd look at *my* workload. Maybe I could give them 10 hours off of my workload.

Typically, my goal was to at least find 50% billable time to hand over to a new employee. If I'm paying them a full-time salary, I had enough work for them to recoup half of that. Then I knew I had to cover the other half. You usually can't find a full 40 hours of billable work to just hand off to somebody, but you can find *some* billable hours for them. My point is, you don't keep your contractors doing their work and then hire another employee and try to start them from scratch. You're going to be floating that person's salary for a time as you try to get them clients. The strategy is to tell your contractors, "Look, I've been getting so busy, I've had to hire somebody. Unfortunately, I'm going to have to take these clients off of you and give them to my employee."

Again, I would typically give my employees 40% to 50% billable time right off the bat. Well, guess what. If you got to float the other 50% of that person's salary, what better motivator to get more work than to know you're basically paying somebody in your company to sit around and do nothing? That would eat me up inside. So, I busted my butt to go get more clients!

I never expected that any employee is 100% billable. That's just not feasible or reasonable. There's going to be admin time. There are going to be other things they're going to do that aren't billable so I would shoot for 70% or preferably 80%

billable time. The other 10% to 20% is going to be admin time, breaks, lunches, and things like that. You have to take the time to figure out what metrics work for *your* business.

METRICS

In my company, we ran a lot of metrics. We knew what our gross profit percentage needed to be on all our client work. If our labor cost was X, and we knew we wanted to get 60% gross profit on the job, our retail rate had to be Y, and we had to make sure our labor rates remained at a certain percentage. That's tough to do when you increase wages, and when you increase benefits. You have to figure out ways to delegate work, figure out new processes and workflows to become more efficient because you have to keep that labor rate at a certain percentage. We always ran production metrics. We knew how much billable time and how much non-billable time each employee had. *Remember, each employee has their own P&L,* so we would go through all their clients and make sure the average profitability for that employee was where it needed to be to meet our company goals.

It's very important you develop metrics with your own company. Remember, know your numbers!

Now, back to my new employee at 50% billable time. My contractors are sitting on the sidelines and hungry for more work for the time being, but my first priority was always my employees—*and your first priority should always be your employees and getting them work.* You should not have employees sitting around not doing any work while you're paying a contractor to do the work. You've got to put the contractors on hold, and once I got my employees up to the right production goals (the billable goals), the next work that came in I'd give to my contractor.

You can see my hiring and delegation pattern. I loaded up contractors, contractors, contractors, and once I had enough work to hire a new employee, I'd get them to about 40% or 50% billable time, moving all that work to the new employee. Then with the next round of new work that came in, I would load up the new employee until they got to their utilization rate which was usually around 80% or a little higher. Once we got the new employee to that rate, when new work came in we went back to the contractors and loaded them appropriately.

Once we got to the point where we had enough billable work between our contractors, we would hire another employee, take the work off the contractors, give it to the employee and go through the same cycle.

Contractors are a great solution and resource to scale your business. You just have to be upfront with them and say, "We're going to continue to utilize you this way. This is why you're here. We're going to do everything in our power to keep you busy and take care of your needs." They're great for solving workload issues, and for crises. During tax season, for example, you need extra bodies to do the work. Contractors are a great resource for that. And, on occasion, you might turn one of your contractors into a full-time employee. We did that a couple times when there was a contractor we really liked who worked well within our system. Typically, something happens in their life that allows them to go full time. In one case, we had a mom whose kids got to a point where she didn't need to be home all the time with them, so she decided to go from contractor to full-time employee and that was great. That employee had worked with me as a contractor for years and now we were able to provide her with the opportunity to go full time. I think that's a great thing, if you can offer those opportunities to your contractors.

DAN STEINER

You can convert a decent number of contractors into employees. It's almost a test drive of them, to make sure they're good; but contractors are usually contractors for a reason. They do what their capacity allows them to. Usually, it's personal reasons, but if those personal reasons change, you need to stay in touch with them and say, "Look, if at any point in time you can give me more hours or you can go full time, please let me know. I want to be the first one to have the opportunity to hire you for my company."

Keep that in mind as you're building your network of contractors.

SCALE

That's how I initially scaled my business. That's how I grew organically. When you bring on a new employee, you should be able to get them to a certain percentage of billable time. I wouldn't suggest you hire an employee unless they've got a certain amount of billable time you've already got lined up for them. You're going to have to cover the rest of their salary that your clients aren't paying for and that's what you might use a line of credit for. On a couple of occasions, I've used my credit line to float an employee. Usually it wouldn't be more than a month or two because we were very fortunate that we were getting new clients consistently. I knew a short-term funding solution like a line of credit would be invaluable to help me bridge that gap to get an employee to the right utilization percentage.

94

BE A CEO

The other thing you're going to have to understand is that you, the business owner, is not going to get a raise for quite a bit of time. You're going to have to understand there's a slim chance you're going to be able to put money away for retirement the traditional way. Some business owners go years without being able to pay themselves anything. By the time I grew my business to the point where I could give myself a raise, that was the exact point I needed to hire another person. For years it was almost like clockwork that as soon as I had enough discretionary money where I could give myself a raise, inevitably, my staff would come to me or I would recognize that we needed to hire somebody. My hard-earned raise ended up going to that new employee to cover that salary until we got them to their production goals. A lot of my raises, instead of taking them, I used them to reinvest in the business.

When we talk about sacrifice and we talk about risk, we are really talking about, *Are you all in, or not?* If you're all in to selling your business for a high value amount, you've got to sacrifice some of your personal financial gains early on and reinvest those into the business. And understand when I say "investment," I'm not talking about a 401K contribution. Instead, you're making a contribution into the retirement fund which *is your business.* You have to psychologically look at it that way and you're probably going to have to explain it to your spouse that way.

I made good money when I worked in the corporate world and you get used to that, your spouse gets used to that. Then you start a business and people on the outside looking in think it's a matter of turning on the faucet, that you keep the same salary you're used to getting. Your spouse doesn't understand why, when you use to make $100,000 a year, you're now making $60,000 a year (for example). That's a hard concept for anyone to swallow, but you're the *owner*. You're in it every day, so you understand what's going on, but your spouse probably doesn't (at least to the same degree). It's critical you communicate with your spouse or significant other regularly about what's going on in your business. You are sacrificing your pay (for now) because you know when you use it to invest in a new employee, when you invest in technology, you invest in new office space—there are lots of different ways you can invest your money in your business, but *that's what you're doing, making an investment.*

Some might decide, "Look, I deserve more. There's no way I should pay myself $50,000, $60,000 a year with all the headaches and stress I'm going through. I deserve *a lot* more. I'm going to start paying myself $100,000 a year because that's what I'm worth." That's fine but that's short sighted. That's going to give you some immediate satisfaction but if you do that, you're going to dramatically slow the growth of your company. If you're paying yourself $100,000, you're not going to have the capital or the cash flow to hire a new employee, you're not going to have the cash flow to take advantage of another opportunity that comes around because you decided you need to make a big salary.

Go as long as you can without taking a raise. I'm not saying you have to stand in bread lines, I'm just saying take only as much as you need to survive or live a realistic lifestyle. Don't be so aggressive with your pay that you limit the opportunities for you to grow. Instead of giving myself a raise, I decided to offer health benefits to my employees, or I decided to do something else for my employees. Ultimately, if you're successful and you run your business the right way, not only will you get the salary you deserve, you're going to get your big payday when you decide to sell your business because you had the foresight and the discipline to reinvest those dollars in your business.

That's really how I was able to grow. It's all about *managing*. That's the key word and we preach that to all our clients. It's amazing how a lot of us don't practice what we preach and things get out of hand because we don't have the discipline. You have to manage and you have to be disciplined. You constantly have to understand the workload and you have to juggle several balls in the air at the same time. You can't focus all your attention on sales because you're so hungry for clients, because if you focus all your energy on sales and business development and you're not out there looking for contractors or employees, what are you going to do with all those new clients? If your business development efforts are successful, it doesn't mean a thing if you don't have anybody to do the work.

You have to be very structured and disciplined with how you spend (invest) your time. My advice is you never stop looking for clients and you never stop looking for employees. That never ever stops unless you're ready to quit. You should never stop because you can't simply turn the faucet on and off. You just can't say, "Oh, okay, I'm not going to look for clients for a while because we're doing pretty good." You can't do that because you and I both know you could lose half a dozen clients or more over the period of one quarter. If you stop your business development efforts, then that's going to have a big impact on your business. I never stopped my business development efforts and I always figured out a way to get the work done.

You can work around the clock for years, but as you grow as the CEO, you're not going to be able to maintain that—your other responsibilities (including management) are going to start taking up more time. As I grew, I stopped doing as much of the bookkeeping work as I had been. I was much more particular about the work that I did as the CEO. I started taking on more of the high-level, high-value client work, whether that was consulting or CFO/Controller work or some of the nastier cleanup work because I knew if I gave it to someone who wasn't qualified enough to do that cleanup work, it would take them three times as long as it would take me to do it. I didn't feel comfortable charging the client for three times the hours because I gave the work to somebody who wasn't suited to do that kind of work.

It was important I evaluated the jobs that came in and made sure they went to the right people. I was able to start handpicking the work that I did. It got more and more like that over time until I only worked with a few select clients myself. I got to a point where I wasn't doing any more bookkeeping work. My role as CEO started to develop into mainly marketing, business development, and developing my managers. When you are more focused on building the value of your firm you are going to have to step out of a production role and get more into a manager or CEO role, where it's important you get the right people in your firm, you train them the right way, and you build your brand.

I handled a lot of the metrics and analytics of profitability. My job as the CEO was to make sure that the business was profitable, that I was building a valuable business that I knew I could sell down the road. I didn't start hiring managers early on. I knew I could manage several people at a time before I had to bring somebody in at a manager level because those folks are going to cost a lot more money. That's a bigger investment.

DELEGATION

Be honest with yourself. I say that a lot, but you need to recognize when too much is too much. You don't want to be too proud and think, *I got this,* when really, you should delegate. Business owners and entrepreneurs usually have a lot of control issues. *There's nothing scarier than handing over a piece of your business to somebody else.* There are some tasks I didn't let go of. For example, through the life of my business, I have done my own books, from paying bills to bank reconciliations. I am the only check signer in the company, I always have been. I felt that was the best way to stay on the pulse of the company.

As we got bigger and bigger and we were getting into hundreds of thousands of dollars in revenue with 100 to 200 clients, it seemed very easy to lose control of what was going on. Doing the books (and payroll) myself was my way to keep my eyes on what was going on. I brought in managers to manage the staff. I identified early on that managing large numbers of people was not my expertise. I didn't get much enjoyment out of it. I knew I needed to bring in people who could help manage my staff of bookkeepers.

I knew I couldn't be in communication with all my clients. For the first however many years, I knew every single client and every client knew me. I knew them on a personal level, I knew their names, I knew all the work we were doing for them. But it gets to a point where that just can't happen. You just can't touch every single client. You've got to have people in your company who can do that, and you move more to a higher level of overview. I stayed in touch with clients as best I could, but you can't touch all of them all the time.

To grow, you're going to have to delegate. You are going to have to get people. It's easy to delegate the bookkeeping work, but trickier at the management level. I didn't hire my first manager *as a manager*. I hired him initially as a QuickBooks trainer when I started my QuickBooks training division. As he worked more and more with me, he ended up developing into my operations manager. My second manager came about through an acquisition.

You don't want to be too quick to hire. I certainly had a high threshold of pain. I was willing to work crazy hours before I brought in somebody. But at some point, you have to recognize that you only have so much bandwidth to keep things under control. Whether you develop an employee from inside your company to be a manager (i.e. promote from within), or you hire somebody from the outside, it's critical you identify when the right time is to bring in a manager. I knew which duties I didn't want to do anymore, and that's how I would approach hiring. I knew my strengths. You need to understand your strengths and your weaknesses and, as I said a hundred times, be honest with yourself. What are you good at? What things are most critical to you? What things can you offload? Answer these questions and you'll feel okay about replacing yourself in the appropriate areas.

Before I hired a manager, I made a list—"Here's what I will not let go of no matter what. I've got the Kung Fu grip on this stuff and nobody's going to take it!" Then I made a list of things I wanted to offload, those things I didn't enjoy doing every day anymore, but would love if somebody took off my plate. In fact, that's how you develop your job descriptions, and that helps you identify who the ideal candidates are going to be. Then you need to go out there and find yourself a manager.

How are you going to pay for that? Well, that manager is probably going to get *your raise*. You're probably going to get to the point where you've got a full staff of bookkeepers and one or more managers in place before you're going to get yourself to a salary or compensation level that you're comfortable with. But I'd rather invest that raise (that I would have gotten myself) into a manager because that manager is *an investment*, and you're taking the time and things they do *off of your plate*. It's going to free you up to do other things like business development. As much as hiring adds a big line item expense on your P&L, you need to look at it as an asset. I knew if I wasn't going to get a raise, at least I was going to put that money into somebody who could help me manage this business and take a lot of time and responsibility off my plate.

DUE DILIGENCE

You need to hire people who have relevant and current skillsets. It's critical you perform skill tests on potential hires to determine if they know how to do the work and use the necessary software. That's part of your brand. I was willing to pay people a little bit more, above market rate, but I wanted good, solid people because my reputation was on the line. It's important you hire people who know what they're doing and, particularly, that they understand QuickBooks software since that's the leading accounting software today. I've learned that lesson the hard way, hiring contractors and employees whose resumes said one thing and when you actually get them in the seat and you tell them, "Here you go, let's get started!" they don't know how to use Excel or some other critical program.

"Oh, I used QuickBooks eight years ago but I haven't seen *this* version before," they say. Hmm, interesting. Can you see my eyes rolling?

It's hard to fully comprehend how turnover impacts a business. Nobody wants a lot of turnover. I speak from experience. Losing just one person can have an impact that ripples through your company. The reality is you're going to have turnover. We talked about risk, and that's one of the big risks. One of the things that kept me up at night was wondering when I came to the office the next day, was I going to have a voicemail or email or somebody sitting in my office telling me they were quitting, or one of my managers telling me somebody had quit. That was devastating news. That's not something any business owner wants to walk into, but you need to be prepared for that. You need to mitigate that risk by putting the effort into hiring good people. That involves background checks and skill tests. Do your due diligence on your employees.

Do your due diligence when it comes to pay as well. You have to constantly evaluate where you are in the market because if you're paying people below market or you're not offering benefits and everybody else in the market is, you're at risk of losing your employees at any time. I worried I was going to have people quit or leave to go work for a competitor so it's important you know that your employee is in a good place. If you know your local job market, and an employee comes to you for a raise, you don't have to just say okay. You could tell them, "Look, I know what the market is. I know what I'm paying you is good. You've got a good job. I don't know there are a lot of better options out there. If you want to go test the market, go for it, but I think you're in a pretty good place here."

This gives business owners a lot of confidence when they're talking to employees (or potential employees) about wages. I would push back if I needed to push back. If I had a particular job and I knew I could only charge the client $50 an hour, I knew I had to go find a contractor to do that work for X amount of dollars in order to get my gross profit the right way. You've got to have a handle on your labor rates. It also helps to know you have options when hiring. You might approach a contractor and ask, "What's your rate?"

"Well," they say, "it's $30 an hour."

If this is the only person you're talking to and you are not solid on what the market pays, you're beholden to that one bookkeeper and it will affect the gross profit on all your clients. Because I know the market, what I would do is say, "Well, that's high, because if my average price to clients is $50 an hour, you at $30 an hour doesn't leave me enough margin to make the profit that I need to make. You either need to lower your hourly fee or I'm going to have to find somebody else who can do that work for the rate I need."

If they want to stay at $30, that's their choice, but I always like to have two or three other options available to me. If I'm doing my job as the owner, I'm going to be able to put my hands on a contractor who bills me the rate I need, so I'm able to charge that customer what I need to charge them.

Don't put all your eggs in one basket. Don't be beholden to any one contractor. As a business owner, it's important you're always recruiting as many contractors as you can put your hands on because they're going to have their own limitations. It's not always a matter of their rate, it could be what part of the city they're going to go to, what days they're going to be able to work, what hours they're going to be able to work, and so on. Don't just say, "I found a contractor," and, "What's your rate?" because that person is going to now dictate margins for your entire business and what you can charge your customers.

When hiring, as with anything else, you have to be smart. Analyze. Every decision is a risk-reward. At the end of the day, you want to be profitable, so always consider a few things:

- With this client coming in, can I be profitable?
- Do I have the right person in my company to do this work?

- If I bring them on, am I going to make a reasonable gross profit?

It's important these considerations go into your decisions on hiring employees and contractors.

[7] IDENTIFYING NEW REVENUE STREAMS

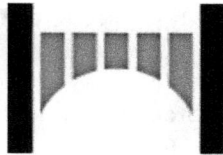

SYNERGY

*I*DENTIFYING NEW STREAMS *of revenue* is critical. It's an effective way to scale your business. There's nothing to say you can't grow a strictly bookkeeping service business into a multi-million-dollar business, but it's a lot tougher that way. Bookkeeping is, typically, fairly low-revenue, low-margin work. You have to engage with a lot of clients to get a sizable book of business. My strategy with Steiner Business Solutions was to start off with bookkeeping. It was the need I identified in the market, and it's a fairly low-cost, low-barrier-to-entry-type of service, especially when you're just trying to get your name out there. Even though I was qualified to do higher level work, I knew people didn't know me outside of my employer, they didn't know I existed, and you don't have the trust or the credibility to back it up.

Bookkeeping is something all small business owners understand. You don't have to do a whole lot of explaining of what it is that you do. I noticed the majority of help wanted ads on Craigslist were for part-time bookkeeping services. Back then, outsourced bookkeeping by itself was not a well-known commodity, and that's why I got into that type of business. Also, there was hardly any contract CFO work being done at the time. Even staffing companies weren't placing many part-time CFOs. Knowing those services would require a lot of explaining to business owners, meant I probably wouldn't close a lot of business, so I decided to start with bookkeeping and then work my way up.

When I first started Steiner Business Solutions, 95% of the work was bookkeeping. In 2010, a good percentage of my bookkeeping clients were asking me if I could do their taxes. Doing taxes is not something I was really interested in, so I farmed it out to a CPA I knew in town, whom I trusted, and he did a good job. It got to the point where I was sending him 20 or 30 tax returns a season. I could have kept doing that, but you have to think about how you might take advantage of a situation like that. I didn't like the idea of sending my clients to another CPA who more than likely, if he wasn't doing it then, eventually would start offering his own bookkeeping service.

He already had access to my clients, as he was doing their taxes. What's to stop him from saying, "Hey, we already do your taxes. Why don't you let us do your bookkeeping work?" It was a two-pronged thought for me—*I'm giving up all this revenue to somebody else. Why don't I keep it?* And, *Here I am giving clients to a competitor of mine!* It didn't make good business sense to me so I decided I was going to start my own tax business. I formed a separate LLC for my tax business, which is called Steiner Tax Services, for a number of reasons:

1. I wanted to make sure I had a true accounting of my businesses, and it's easier to manage when the books are separate.
2. I knew down the road if I wanted to sell my tax business for whatever reason, it would make it a lot cleaner transaction if it was legally separate. I wouldn't *have to* split it off from my accounting business, it would just be a cleaner sale.
3. I wasn't doing the taxes myself, so I had to find somebody to do them. When you're just starting out, particularly in the tax business, CPAs are rather expensive. How was I going to convince a CPA who wants to make $100,000 a year to come help me? Having a separate tax business allowed me to offer equity in that company as an incentive for a CPA to join me.

I've never had to offer equity, but that was certainly an option I considered had I found someone who could take charge and grow my tax business. I always knew I could offer equity in Steiner Tax Services without giving up any ownership in Steiner Business Solutions.

That's pretty forward thinking, right? *I mean, before I even decided to start my tax company, I was already thinking through the exit strategy.* I was already thinking, *How can I find good people? How can I retain good people to work in my tax business?* It was a struggle. I went through three or four contractors before I grew the tax business to a point where it was producing enough revenue to pay somebody a decent salary and have them stay.

The point is I identified an additional revenue stream. I thought to myself, *How can I keep this tax work in house so I can benefit from this revenue source instead of giving it away to somebody?* Instead of saying, "Okay, I'll now add tax services to Steiner Business Solutions," I was forward-thinking and thought, *It's better to track the tax services in a different set of books, and what if I want to offer equity in the company? This is a great way to attract and or retain my tax manager down the road. And if I wanted to sell the tax business, it was a nice, clean transaction and easy to calculate the value, so forth and so on.* That was the first additional revenue stream I brought on.

Once I started my tax business I was able to pivot on my marketing. I advise people to find what differentiates them from the competition, and there I was, a bookkeeping company which *also* offered to do your taxes. That was a competitive edge I had against other bookkeepers who weren't doing taxes. My marketing pitch started to be, "Would you like to have the same company doing your books and your taxes?"

Even though they were two separate LLCs legally, I didn't promote Steiner Tax Services as its own entity. For example, I didn't have a separate web page for Steiner Tax Services. The invoices we sent to our clients read *Steiner Tax Services* on them, but all my marketing was integrated. Even my Steiner Business Solutions website had a separate page for taxes, but the consumer didn't know it was a separate LLC. Quite honestly, I don't know that anyone would have cared, but it made the marketing much easier for me. So, at that point, I was promoting that I could do everything under one roof. That created an additional revenue stream for me. It also offered the ability to change my message to, "We're different than the other bookkeeping companies. Get it all done under one roof."

If you don't have another revenue stream outside of bookkeeping, you might offer tax services. There was a good bit involved in how I pulled this off, but it is possible, of course. You're probably going to have to go through a few people to finally get the tax business large enough that it actually spins off a decent amount of revenue. Fortunately today I do make a decent paycheck off my tax business. It's grown to a decent size business that is valuable enough that if I wanted to sell it, I could.

MORE SYNERGY

The next revenue stream I brought on was QuickBooks training. A lot of small business owners do the books themselves, and most of them aren't very good at it or they don't really have the time to do it. One of the objections we got for bookkeeping services was, "I can do this myself so I don't know why I would pay you a lot of money to do it. It's probably not that hard." As I said, business owners often devalue bookkeeping. So, instead of losing that customer because they didn't want to pay me, even if it's just a couple hundred bucks a month to do their bookkeeping, I wanted to figure out how I could still keep that customer. I decided to start offering QuickBooks training!

At first, we started with a classroom format of up to 12 people. We tried that for a few months, but it ended up where we just couldn't get enough people in the seats to make it worthwhile. The classes ran most of the day, but we found business owners did not want to sit in a classroom for five hours or more a day, learning 12 chapters of QuickBooks. We ended up developing a new business plan. We moved more to customized one-on-one training where we only trained the client on the modules that were relevant to the client's day-to-day business. We added the QuickBooks training service because I needed to capture a new source of revenue. If I couldn't acquire them as a bookkeeping client, I wanted to at least capture them as a QuickBooks *student*. "Give yourself a fighting chance to get it done right," we said. We charged $250 for a couple hours of training. It was a way to get them into our system at a fairly low cost, giving them exposure to my company and staff.

It gave people an opportunity to experience working with us and not only did we create QuickBooks training revenue but a very high percentage—say 60% to 70%—of the business owners we trained usually ended up coming back to us and asked us to do their bookkeeping. They ended up selling themselves on the value of our bookkeeping services. When they first approached us we explained, "Hey, we'd love to do your bookkeeping. It's $200 a month," but at that point they don't know us or perhaps understand what goes into bookkeeping. They might have thought it was simple to do, or that it takes no time at all.

"No, thank you," they'd say.

"Well," we'd say, let us train you and you do it, then."

Inevitably, they would try it on their own and struggle or forget to do it and get behind. Meanwhile, we had already reached out to them, and they now knew us. They had our contact information, and they liked us. When things started getting behind or they got frustrated, they were ready to sign up for our bookkeeping service! It took all the sales pressure off. We didn't have to sell them anything. They were coming to us saying, "I want to sign up for your bookkeeping services. Please!"

It ended up being a revenue generator for us on two fronts:

1. They paid us $250 for the training;
2. Several months later they often hired us to do their books.

They would go from a $250 one-time fee to a $200 a month bookkeeping client. Then there's the opportunity to tell them about our tax services: "Oh, do you know that we do tax preparation as well?"

"Oh, no, I didn't know that!"

A very high percentage of our bookkeeping clients ended up having us do their taxes, all from getting them through the QuickBooks training. That's how you grow your revenue! The one-and-done client is fine, but if you can do three-to-one, that's higher and faster growth. Now I had QuickBooks training, I had bookkeeping, and I had tax preparation. I have basically captured these business owners from start to finish. At this stage in my business, I had found three different ways to get revenue from the same client.

GROWTH STRATEGY

The analogy I've always used to explain my company's growth strategy is it's kind of like professional baseball. Baseball has four different levels: single A, double A, triple A, and the major leagues. You rarely see players who go straight to the major leagues. They usually start in single A or double A. I looked at clients and small businesses the same way and I put them into categories:

- There is the startup business or someone who has been in business maybe a year or two. That's a *single A*, small business. The owner is probably a sole proprietor.
- As they grow their revenue more significantly and begin to add employees they move up to a *double A,* small business.

I wanted to capture these businesses at an early stage, and then be "sticky" with them. You want to build loyalty at an early stage because the cost of acquisition, when they're that young, is a whole lot cheaper than it is once they're a bigger company with millions in revenue and 50 plus employees. That's when EVERYBODY notices them. They become a much more attractive target for CPA firms and other accounting firms at those numbers.

The startup, however, they're doing $50,000 a year, $75,000 a year, maybe $100,000 a year, and the CPA firms turn their noses up at those businesses. Nobody really wants to work with them because the fees aren't going to be high. But these business owners still need help. I thought, *Well, you know what, if nobody else is going after those clients, I'm going to go after those clients.* Maybe three to five years after they've been working with me, they might be at a million-dollar plus revenue with a bunch of employees. They're now in the major leagues! And guess what, they're going to stick with me, right? I've already captured them at an early stage and they're loyal to me. Now, when they're bigger, I can offer them perhaps fractional CFO or controller services. Their business has gotten more complicated. They might have multiple departments. They've got a lot of employees. They're looking to expand. They're starting to do budgets and forecasts and they're starting to get more sophisticated in their business operations.

At that point I start telling them about my controller services, my CFO services, and my business consulting services. I've got bookkeepers on staff who are going to continue to help these clients with their bookkeeping, but now, Dan is going to offer them his consulting and higher-end services, obviously, for a higher fee. And, that's great for the client! A win-win situation! The client doesn't have to go outside of the Steiner brand to find that level of help. I always marketed and promoted that we could help you at any stage of your business. We have bookkeepers, we have controllers, and we have tax/CPA people. There's no reason why you need to go outside of the Steiner brand to hire another professional. Basically, you can never outgrow us!

Some clients get to a point where outsourcing their bookkeeping doesn't make much sense anymore. They're going to have to hire somebody in-house. Guess who's going to help them do that. That's right, Steiner Business Solutions is going to help them do that. We've worked with that company for however long a time and we've basically built their accounting department. We understand all their processes and workflows—in fact we've likely developed them! When it's time that outsourcing part-time doesn't make sense anymore for them, when they want to hire somebody in-house, we offer to recruit and hire for them. You guessed it, that's *another* revenue stream that I have built! I've had my own clients pay me to help them hire a full-time bookkeeper to replace our part-time person. We'll run the ad, we'll interview and screen all the candidates. We'll put the top two or three candidates in front of the owner and we'll let the owner make the final decision.

Once that person is hired, that person has to be trained, right? Who's going to do that? Steiner Business Solutions is going to do that! Who else better to train the new full-time bookkeeper than the bookkeepers that were there before them? Now we've got *training* revenue to get their in-house person up to speed. Now we need somebody to supervise their in-house person. Who's going to do that? Well, it's not going to be the owner because he or she doesn't really know what's going on in the accounting department. He or she doesn't have the time or the ability to supervise an in-house bookkeeper. So, who's going to do that? That's right. Steiner Business Solutions is going to do that! We're going to do that as part of our controller services.

CONTROLLER SERVICES

The client graduated from having a part-time bookkeeper to a full-time bookkeeper. You would think if you're a bookkeeping company and that's all you do is bookkeeping, that you just lost that client. You no longer have any more revenue from that client. That's a risk. At some point, your clients are going to grow, and when they do, it's going to make sense for them to bring in a full-time bookkeeper. I saw that as a problem. I hate to invest all that time in a client and then they outgrow me. What can I do to prevent a client from outgrowing my services? Well, let's start offering the services above the bookkeeper level. Those are the controller-type services. If a client ever did outgrow me at the bookkeeper level, I can then say, "Okay, client, we found you your in-house, full-time bookkeeper. Now, we're going to supervise and train that bookkeeper and we'll fill that gap between the bookkeeper and you, Mr. Owner or Mrs. Owner." We then develop a whole new revenue stream of controller services.

Just another way that client never outgrew us.

CFO WORK

Along with controller services, we offer higher-level CFO support. We have clients with full-time accounting staff, and we supplement them and work alongside them providing fractional CFO services, which is much more a strategic type of consulting. You're really working directly with the owner on financial strategies, and operational initiatives. We now can work with multi-million-dollar businesses. Again, you're not going to outgrow us. In fact, by the time a client got to the controller or CFO stage, they've probably worked with us for five or six years. By that time, you're practically a part of the team. The owner is so reliant on your expertise, you literally become a part of management. You're not going to lose that client unless you really mess something up.

You evolve and grow to a level where the owner relies on your advice. And who else knows the business better than you do? Are they going to bring in another person they have to train? No, they're not going to do that. They want somebody in there who has worked alongside them for years. That's really what made my business effective. It provided additional revenue, it provided excellent client retention, and it increased the value of my brand. I had all these services under one roof and increased my reputation. I had very minimal client turnover because there was no reason for them to leave.

You have to look for these opportunities, and that's how you're going to grow. That's how you're going to increase your client retention. That's how you're going to increase your brand awareness. You have to listen to your clients. What do they need? Talk to them!

PEER GROUP

The most recently added revenue stream within Steiner Business Solutions is a CEO peer group. I call it *Executive Round Table*. When I sold my bookkeeping division we had over 200 clients in it. I've worked with hundreds and hundreds of clients over my 12 years with Steiner Business Solutions, and that's a lot of learning. That's a lot of real-world experience. I'd heard of peer groups before and I thought this was a great opportunity to expand my offerings and give back to the small business community.

With my peer group, we gather a group of 10-12 business owners together once a month. We meet in my conference room or virtually. We do workshops, mastermind sessions, book reviews, goal setting, and host guest speakers on relative topics. The owners come to learn. A *mastermind session* is where we dig into a challenge or opportunity that particular business owner is facing. We often spend well over an hour dissecting the situation and then give advice and feedback to help that owner make the best decision possible. It's a very good opportunity to have your own board of advisors. I REALLY enjoy that kind of work. I hesitate to even call it work.

SUMMARY

At the end of my corporate career, I was a high-level financial executive. When I started Steiner Business Solutions, I provided bookkeeping services at $15 hour, but I knew that wasn't where I was going to get stuck. It's important *you* don't get stuck, either. You want to be thinking about all the different challenges you're going to face, all the different risks I've pointed out, asking how you are going to overcome and mitigate those risks and grow. I went from working a ton of hours, building a bookkeeping client base, to now, where I pick and choose a handful of clients I work with on advisory services. I was able to sell my bookkeeping business, which was the foundation of my company, and it didn't impact my income. I still make as much money now as I did when I had my bookkeeping business because I've been able to parlay that bookkeeping business into higher-level work, often with many of the clients who started with me as bookkeeping clients. By now, they've all moved up to the major leagues. They've grown their businesses as I've grown my business.

I've established myself as a small business expert and people come knocking on my door. That's the mindset you need to have. I know you don't want to do bookkeeping the rest of your life. It's challenging to do that kind of busy work for years and years. And there's not a lot of money in it unless you can build it to a size I built mine to.

That's the key takeaway. I sold my bookkeeping division for over a million dollars. That's hard to do if you're *just* providing bookkeeping services and not pursuing aggressive growth strategies. I also wouldn't have been able to retain my company, the brand, and continue to do consulting if I hadn't built the consulting, advisory and CFO business *while I was doing the bookkeeping work*. That was all part of my exit strategy; that I could get above market value on the sale of my bookkeeping division, and focus just on the work I really enjoy, and work the hours that I want to work.

That's what I want for *you*, that you get to the point where you've been so strategic with how you build your business that you have options. I had the option of selling my entire company, but I didn't want to sell my entire company. I don't want to stop working. I just wanted to stop doing bookkeeping. I didn't want to have 20-plus employees and what goes with that, so I created options for myself so I could sell my bookkeeping division, keep my brand, keep my company name, and continue to provide valuable services to my clients.

What I want for you is that you can produce so many revenue streams it creates options for you. I still have my tax business. If I wanted to, at any time, I could sell that tax business, or I could bring on a partner. I'm still leaving myself options for what I want to do in the future. All of this was through *forward thinking*. All of this was through evaluating my risk and building multiple revenue streams. If, for whatever reason, I lost a bunch of bookkeeping clients, I still had my QuickBooks training, I still had my tax services, I still had my controller services. You don't want to get too reliant on any one revenue stream.

If you're not capable or you don't have the education or the background to offer some of these consulting services, you could possibly partner up with somebody, or maybe there's a person who would work for you on a contract basis. But just because you don't have the ability yourself to do the work doesn't mean you can't figure out a way to offer it through your company. The perfect example is my tax business. I don't do taxes. I don't want to do taxes. I probably can't do taxes. I figured out a way to have somebody else do the taxes, but it ran through my company. No different than the QuickBooks training. As long as you're a good bookkeeper, you should offer QuickBooks training. I identified that I was losing bookkeeping clients because people thought the price was too high and said they were going to do it themselves. So, I came up with a solution. *How do I convert that person into a client if my bookkeeping services are too high?* That's what brought our QuickBooks training about.

Take a minute and think about your business. You cannot get caught in the day-to-day grind of running a business so much that you lose sight of all the opportunities that are out there.

Think about your bookkeeping clients as a focus group. After all, what better focus group than your own clients to ask, "What else can we do for you?" or, "What do you think the market is missing?" Bookkeeping, for me, was a springboard to higher-value clients. And that's what I want for you—build your credibility, build your brand, and look for other, higher-value revenue streams.

[8] GROWTH STRATEGY ~ ORGANIC VERSUS ACQUISITION

ORGANIC GROWTH

THE GOAL OF THIS BOOK is to help business owners *think through* your growth strategies. What do you want out of your business? There's nothing wrong with keeping yourself small but this book is geared, really, to people who want to build up a large value in their business and then cash out at the end.

What do I mean by *organic* growth? Organic growth is simply getting clients one at a time. When you start your business, you start with that first client, and work your way up.

It's a day-to-day grind of business development, getting one client after another. In the bookkeeping world, if you add 10 clients, you're going to lose four, or you can add three clients and you're going to lose two. If you're fortunate, you're going to add more clients than you lose, but your growth trajectory is going to be fairly flat because you only have so much capacity to add one client at a time. That's what we mean by *organic* growth.

Unfortunately, you're not likely going to build a book of business that's worth a million dollars or more this way. You'd have to accumulate that revenue number over the course of something like 20 years or more, and I'm not here to teach you how to cash out after that many years. My goal is for you to be able to do this much quicker. Organic growth will get you a decent-size book of business, it's not going to get you a large payout when you decide to exit.

MILESTONES

I made my first acquisition five years into my company's existence and I would say by that time I was probably doing about $100,000 to $125,000 in annual revenue. Not a crazy number, right? After five years of being in business, $100,000 in revenue may sound good to a lot of people, but remember, I didn't get to keep $100,000 of that revenue. In fact, I was taking home *far less* than $100,000. Before I started my bookkeeping business, I was making at least $100,000 a year in salary. Five years into business and I was nowhere near where I needed to be income-wise, personally. This gives you an idea of the timeline it took me just to get to about $100,000 in total revenue. And that was probably 95% bookkeeping revenue. That's what I mean by *organic growth*.

The question is, *Do you have a growth strategy? How big is big enough?* These were questions I always grappled with.

- Your first growth milestone with your business should be for your business to generate enough revenue that you can pay yourself a *decent* salary.
- Your next growth milestone should be that your business generates enough revenue that you're able to pay yourself a *high* salary, a *successful* salary, a salary that you set a goal for.

A lot of people stop there, and there's nothing wrong with stopping there. That's a good *job*. But you could probably do that just by getting a job somewhere else, couldn't you? What's the point of generating this awesome business if you're going to stop at creating a nice job for yourself?

Is this business a job to you, or is this business an asset to you—a retirement asset that you're going to sell? If so, push through your business growth goal of simply paying yourself a nice salary.

The next growth milestone should be that you want to double the size of your business every three to four years. I knew I was going to grow my business through *acquisition*, that I wanted this business not just to be a job but to be my retirement vehicle. I encourage you to think through your growth strategy, think through a budget or forecast you might do one year out, five years out, 10 years out, 20 years out. But remember, just like anything, as much as you plan to do things at a certain time, opportunities pop up when you least expect them. That's what happened to me, but I had my eyes open for them. And when I found opportunities, I didn't waste any time taking advantage of them.

ACQUISITIONS

To get *to a business valuation of a million-plus dollars,* you need to achieve consistent high level growth. This more than likely means you're going to have to do some acquisitions. I did my first acquisition in 2012. I bought a company called A&B Financial Services. The owner was semi-retiring and looking for someone to take over. He didn't place an ad or anything, I simply got word through a referral. This is a perfect example of how your network works for you. I had a gentleman in my network who knew me, knew my business, and he told me about a man interested in selling his business. I had let it be known through my network that I was interested in acquisitions. One introduction led to another, and I ended up closing on that deal in 2012. With that first deal I *doubled* my business. I went from $100,000 to about $200,000 in revenue and added employees.

At the time, a $200,000 business was very exciting to me. Having employees was exciting to me. The transaction taught me a lot of lessons. Every acquisition you do should teach you a lesson, but I learned *a lot* from this first acquisition. After that first acquisition, I ended up doing a couple more smaller ones.

One smaller acquisition came through one of my employees. Her mother worked as a receptionist at another CPA firm, and that CPA died unexpectedly. My employee's mother told my receptionist. My receptionist told me. I ended up going to the husband and buying her book of business. It wasn't a large business; in fact, it was small enough that I could write a check off my line of credit. Remember what I said earlier in the book, lines of credit are great to have because you never knew when an opportunity is going to come along. In this case I had to act fast. This gentleman didn't know what to do with his wife's business. He wanted to make sure her clients had a place to go. I didn't take on any employees, but I gained a handful of clients. I added more revenue to my book. I'm now adding clients through acquisitions which could have taken me years to acquire, organically. It was my way to multiply my growth, and it was a good way. If I got bookkeeping clients through an acquisition, there was a good opportunity I would also end up getting them as tax clients!

One of the benefits other than getting clients through these acquisitions is you're also getting employees. How hard is it to find employees these days? It's very hard. You're going to go through a lot of interviews. It's very time consuming. It can be very costly to constantly hire people. Through acquisitions you can find clients and employees at the same time. You build your personnel headcount and you build your client headcount exponentially through acquisition versus organic growth.

My next acquisition happened after a local CPA reached out to me. Again, I had put it out there to my network that I was in the market, actively looking for acquisition opportunities. It's no different than trying to get clients—You just can't sit behind your desk and not talk to your network. Your network needs to work for you. I didn't place any ads that I was looking to buy companies, I just told everybody in my network.

Somehow this person heard of me, and they sent me an email that said, "Hey, I'm getting back into the corporate world. I ran my accounting business for a few years and it's just not for me. Would you be interested in buying my book of business?" There were no employees with this one. It was purely clients.

I said, "Sure, I'll take a look at it" and ended up closing on the deal after a short due diligence period. It wasn't a massive acquisition, but they were solid clients. The fees were even more than what I was charging, and that's very important, that the fees match up. If you acquire a company and their fees are much lower than yours, and you try to implement your fee structure, you're going to lose a lot of those clients. It's critical when you do any type of merger or acquisition that the fee structure is pretty much in line with yours. It's even better if you can find an acquisition where the seller charges their clients more than you charge yours. That's even more of an opportunity to get a higher return on your investment and increase your revenue.

My largest acquisition up to this point was $100,000, but in 2016, I acquired a company called Net30 in Richmond, Virginia, and this one was *big*, far bigger than what I had ever done before. Over the course of nine years I had built a good staff, I had a key manager in place, and I felt I had the infrastructure to take on a big acquisition.

Remember, organic growth is a lot easier to keep up with. It goes back to my strategy on when and how to hire. You bring in work, you hand off that work, you bring in more work, you hand off that work, and so on. It's a very structured, very simplistic way to grow, organically, with a lot less risk. You don't have to take on debt to grow organically, client-by-client, employee-by-employee. But debt is part of the equation when you do acquisitions and you exponentially increase your company's size. In my case I was often doubling the size of my company by doing these acquisitions. By 2019 I had doubled my business twice in a span of three years. I went from $500,000 to a million in annual revenue, and then from $1 million to $2 million. I was doing an acquisition every 12 to 18 months. It stretched our staff and our resources, and it was a lot of hard work.

Before you start taking on acquisitions, you need to be prepared for that. You need to make sure you have the infrastructure to handle your first, second, third, fourth, however many acquisitions you end up doing. Don't go into an acquisition until you feel you can handle it. By "handling," I don't just mean financially, but in terms of your infrastructure as well. You need to have the people in place, you need to have the processes in place, you need to have yourself a business plan of how you plan to incorporate and integrate the new company, how you plan to handle the transition, how you plan to onboard any new employees. It's critical you prepare yourself for taking on all that additional client work and employee labor.

WHEN THE TIME IS RIGHT

Every time I did an acquisition, I did it because I was confident my staff could handle it. When I started doing my larger acquisitions I had a good grip on the market. My business model was pretty much dialed in. We were very profitable and producing consistent cash flow. We were confident in what we were doing. Just adding one client at a time, we felt we weren't really taking advantage of our strong position in the market. I felt it was time to start leveraging our successful business model by aggressively going after market share. I knew there were a lot of small one- or two-person bookkeeping companies out there and these smaller companies were probably going as far as they wanted to go, whereas I was looking to consolidate, to bring them and their clients under my company umbrella. I was looking at listings every day. I had my network out there looking for me and I would scour those broker listings every night, looking for what I thought was a good fit.

It was important when I was out there looking for these acquisition targets, that I was very focused and disciplined on *what* I was looking for. When I did my very first acquisition, the one we discussed at the start of this chapter, I was doing very little tax work. I was focused more on bookkeeping. That company was mostly bookkeeping, but they also did taxes, which was fine. I was looking to make sure the company I acquired included at least somebody who could continue doing taxes.

As I digested that first acquisition, I learned a lot. And that helped me with my next acquisition and my next acquisition. As you grow and you bring on so many diverse clients, you start to define who your ideal client is. Then you start to determine how much of your business you want to be bookkeeping, how much you want it to be tax, how much you want it to be other things. Once I got those smaller acquisitions out of the way, it helped me define what I wanted my next acquisition to be, and I knew I was going to go *bigger*. I would still gobble up as many of the small ones I could, I wouldn't turn them away, but I was starting to look for the bigger ones, too. I was starting to look for $250,000 acquisitions. I was starting to look for $300,000 acquisitions.

I put the word out on the street on what I was looking for. If a listing was more tax heavy than it was bookkeeping, I didn't even look at it. I came up with a service mix ratio. I wouldn't even look at a listing unless the bookkeeping or accounting portion represented at least 60% to 70% of the total revenue, which means the tax could be anywhere from 30% to 40%. I didn't do any auditing. A lot of CPA firms have auditing as part of their revenue mix. If the practice listing had a high percentage of audit revenue, I didn't even look at it. That pre-determined service mix helped me drill down into listings that I was focused on. Once I saw a listing that seemed to have my target mix of services, I reached out to the broker. Instead of going through all the non-disclosure paperwork and the due diligence process, I would ask, "What is the product mix? How much of this business's revenue is coming from bookkeeping and monthly accounting work?" If it didn't meet the threshold, I said, "Thank you very much," and I moved on to the next one. If it did match that service mix, then I proceeded further and deeper into the due diligence process.

Not all acquisitions go the way you think they're going to go. I've had plenty of acquisitions I started on that didn't come to fruition. On one, we made it all the way to the closing table and the day of closing we ended up parting ways and not doing the deal. Acquisitions (in any form or fashion) are not easy. They're very time-consuming. There's a lot of due diligence. There are lawyers going back and forth. You may talk to three, four or five listings before you actually close your first acquisition. They're very risky, which is why I didn't bite off more than I could chew early on.

I knew that first one, which was $100,000, was probably as high as I wanted to go at the time. That was where my comfort level was. I figured I could digest that size of a company. After I did a couple more smaller ones, my confidence continued to grow, and I knew I needed to think bigger! Each new target I set for my next acquisition grew by hundreds of thousands of dollars.

That's how I grew my business from the first client to a $2 million business. I continually did acquisitions and I pushed my people. It was important they knew where I wanted to go with this business and that I had the confidence in them. They needed to step up and become good managers, run our processes, run our systems. I knew it would be a lot of work and we all worked really hard. We definitely had some challenges along the way. I'm not going to lie to you. It's not easy but, ultimately, if you want to get to the point where you can retire and have a multi-million-dollar business that you can sell, you're going to have to take some chances and understand what those risks are.

BE READY

I didn't do my first acquisition until I was five years into my business. I started with a fairly small one, but it doubled my size, from $100,000 to $200,000 in revenue. Probably the biggest shakeup was taking on half-a-dozen new employees and trying to integrate them into the business. Before that, I was working out of my house. When I did that first acquisition in 2012, that's when I had my first physical office location. A lot of change, right? You go from a guy who works out of his house and meets clients at Panera to a guy who's got a $200,000 business with six or seven employees in an office space! My credibility started to rise, my name got out into the market, and it was a really good steppingstone.

First SBS office location in 2012

Image © 2020 Dan Steiner

I call that first acquisition my *steppingstone*. That's when people started to take me seriously but, again, that was just the first step of my growth strategy—to get an office location, to get employees, to get my book of business growing. Then you can promote that you did an acquisition. You do a press release and people start saying, "Oh, wow! Who's this Dan Steiner guy? He's out there buying companies." When you put that out there, that's when more opportunities start to come your way. As I mentioned, I had one guy reach out to me and tell me he was looking to sell and get back into the corporate world. The more you put it out there, the more the opportunities are going to show up.

All the while, you continually build your infrastructure, which is your people, your processes, your IT. We ended up buying our own server. We used to host with a third-party vendor, but as we got bigger, we decided to get our own server and host all our own stuff. You want to make sure you've got the technology bandwidth to handle this type of growth.

As mentioned earlier, you've got to define your ideal service mix. In my case, that meant what percentage of revenue needed to be bookkeeping versus tax. It's critically important that you stick to the service mix you can and want to handle.

Then you have to define your buying power. What kind of money can you put your hands on? We talked about lines of credit, and those helped my purchase power. You probably can't buy a $300,000 or $400,000 business on a line of credit, but you can certainly put a down payment on a $300,000 or $400,000 business with your line of credit. If part of your growth strategy is to do acquisitions, you need to start lining up your capital strategy to go along with that. How can you put your hands on the money you're going to need to do these acquisitions? There are different ways, of course.

For one, you could go with a traditional bank loan. I did an SBA loan for my last acquisition, a large acquisition in Wilmington, North Carolina. That was the best lending resource for me for that situation. Other times, you might use a mix of funding. I always recommend you try to get seller financing. And by *seller*, I mean the person you're buying the business from. They know it would be in their best interest to help the buyer have a successful close. Banks aren't typically going to lend 100% of the purchase price. A lot of times the seller will offer terms to help you come up with the funds to make the acquisition. With seller financing, you don't have to jump through as many hoops, typically, to get that kind of lending, whereas a bank, as we all know, is going to make you jump through every hoop they possibly can.

I recommended early in the book that you develop relationships with bankers. This comes back to working your network as best you can. If I have another acquisition coming up, I'm going to look at what cash I have on hand, how much I have available on my line of credit, how much cash I think I could potentially get from a traditional lender, how much money I could get from an investor, and how much money I could get from the seller.

You might know somebody in your network that has some cash. If you know somebody who has money and they're looking for good business opportunities, you might reach out and say, "Hey, I'm looking to acquire this business and I'd love it if you could help fund it." I would try not to give out equity if at all possible but set it up as a loan. They could invest in your business and you could treat them as one of your lenders. It might be a combination. You could end up having three or four sources of capital to help you close on an acquisition.

You typically can't just snap your fingers and *presto,* you've got all these lending resources. These take time to develop.

That should be part of your growth strategy, to build up your funding channels. Constantly talk to your banks. Don't just work with one bank. You might have to get funding from two or three banks and that might be tough because banks always want to be in that first position on any type of loan. You can still shop multiple banks. If you only work with one bank, you've only got one option. I have multiple banking relationships and I would shop them. I'd ask, "Who's going to give me the best deal? Who's going to turn this loan around for me the quickest?" I don't like to drag my feet. I don't like to wait. I'm going to first reach out to the bank that usually gives me less hassle, has less bureaucrat red tape, the one I know is going to get that deal done quickly for me. I want to close on this deal before somebody else gets it.

You have to work on that. You have to carve out time and constantly work your growth strategy. The worst result would be that an opportunity pops up you just have to have but you can't put together the funding. It's important you work on that in advance.

TIMING

Don't go crazy on growth at the risk of jeopardizing your business. Plan, plan, and plan. Your job as the CEO is not to get swept up in the day-to-day grind. Your job is to develop *strategy* for your business. I want you to grow your business to a million dollars. I want you to have the ability to sell your business and put a bunch of cash in the bank so you then can control when you work and decide who you work with. I want you to enjoy financial freedom. I want you to get to a point where this business you're working so hard on is going to give you the retirement you want. So, you have to plan. You have to see it. You have to have the vision this can happen.

There are *so many opportunities* out there for consolidation. One of the service offerings (revenue streams) I've created is a *mergers and acquisitions* (M&A) division, where I help other companies buy and sell businesses. If I have a client and they want to *sell* their business, I consult with them on how to prepare their business for sale. I help them structure and negotiate the deal. I help them review the contract and negotiate the price. I consult with them throughout the entire process. I also do that for people who want to *buy* a business. I help buyers with the due diligence work and determine what a good purchase price would be. I help with the onboarding, transition, and integration of the new company. That's *another* revenue stream I have with my business. How many are we up to? I encourage anyone who reads my book to reach out to me if they would like my help with acquisitions they are working on. Or even how to get started with the process. It always helps to lean on someone who has been through the process before—successfully.

I don't plan to do any more acquisitions - but if I did, I would have a very clear, concise description of exactly what I want my acquisition to look like. I would know the geographical area. I would know the revenue size. I would know the management and staffing needs. I would drill down into all the details to the nth degree. You have to learn from your past experiences so you have clarity on what you're trying to do. It saves you a lot of time and it mitigates your risk. You don't want to "learn" from a million-dollar acquisition. You want to learn from small acquisitions. You're going to learn *different* lessons from a small acquisition than you will from a large acquisition, but believe me, you will be in a much better position to learn from a million-dollar acquisition *after* you've done some smaller ones. Don't make your first acquisition a huge one. Learn from the smaller ones, so if they go bad, you can easily recover from them.

If you go too hard too fast and you take on an acquisition that's beyond your bandwidth, beyond your infrastructure, beyond your lending capabilities or capital capabilities, it could put you out of business. You should start small, learn, and that will help your chances of success on the next one, and on the next one after that. Step out of your comfort zone, continue on your organic growth, but also look for those opportunities for acquisition because they're out there. There are lots of CPAs who are retiring. There are lots of bookkeeping companies, especially the one- or two-person bookkeeping companies. They might get to $100,000 or $200,000 in revenue but then things happen, personal situations arise, they need to get out, they need to sell their business, or some of them lose a bunch of clients and they want to go back and get a more solid, comfortable corporate job. Those opportunities are out there but you're not going to find them unless you put the word out.

You *can* grow your business to a million dollars or more, and you're going to have to do it with a combination of organic growth and acquisitions.

[9] MAXIMIZE THE VALUE OF YOUR BUSINESS

BUILT TO SELL

EARLY ON IN MY BUSINESS, I was introduced to a book written by John Warrillow called *Built to Sell: Creating a Business That Can Thrive Without You*. It's one of those books like *Rich Dad Poor Dad* (by Robert Kiyosaki), that inspired me to launch my own business. *Built to Sell* helped me think through what I wanted my business model to be. I had ideas of how I wanted it to be. I felt confident I knew what services I wanted to provide, but I wondered how to provide them *the right way* because I knew early on that I was looking for an exit strategy. This wasn't just going to be a job, and that book gave me the blueprint, it opened my eyes, not just on how to open up a business, but how also to provide services, and how to seek out certain clients.

It's a must-read because it really gets you to think about your approach. It gives interesting case studies. Ultimately, the biggest takeaway for me was that a *subscription model* was best, that you want to develop some sort of product or service that you can charge every month for. You want recurring revenue, which is consistent, with people coming back. That certainly made sense for bookkeeping. You might get a project where somebody wants you to clean up their books, but ultimately, bookkeeping is a month-to-month arrangement. I was always thinking about how I could do that with my other revenue streams.

I'll give you an example. For our QuickBooks training division, we said, "Yeah, we train people *one time*. It's usually a two-hour training, and then maybe they'll come back for additional training if they get stuck or something, but we'd like to get them on a subscription-type service where we know they're coming back." We thought about creating some kind of video library of short training videos. There are so many topics within QuickBooks it would be easy to build a playlist of YouTube videos and then sell a monthly subscription to that. You don't make it very expensive, but you just keep adding content. Our clients would have an easy, convenient way to get ongoing training and tips. Fresh content is the key. Eventually, if you don't change or add to the content, people aren't going to see any value and they're not going to want to renew. We never got this particular subscription model idea implemented, but we do have a Steiner Business Solutions YouTube page with QuickBooks videos and other useful content.

That's an example of how we tried to create that subscription model within every revenue stream. One of the biggest drivers of the value of your business is if you can create that recurring revenue stream.

I encourage everybody to read *Built to Sell.*

STEPPING AWAY

The *test* if you are going in the right direction with your business is this:

Can you step away from your business for any period of time and have it still run like normal? It doesn't go off the tracks if you're not involved in the day-to-day.

My monthly peer group meeting is only three hours long, but you'd be amazed how many business owners say they can't come to the meeting, not because it was too much money, not because they were intimidated, but simply because they didn't think they could be away from their businesses for *three hours*. I mean, they're telling me, "I'm terrified. I just can't come to the meeting. I can't be out of the loop for three hours." Right there and then, that's all I needed to hear. It means they *really* need to be in that group. We've got to work ON your business so you can be away for three hours. I'm talking about vacations but they're talking about three hours! That response tells me their business is not built to sell. They have not maximized their business because at the end of the day, when a buyer is interested in acquiring you, you're not typically going to be around much longer after the deal closes.

Most of the time, the buyer of a business does not want the seller to come on board. It's important you're able to take a vacation and step away from the business and the business still functions. That's what I use as the test of where you're at.

If you answer the question with, "No, I can't take a vacation," then you need to work on your business at a higher level. Hopefully, you've gotten something out of my chapter of when to hire. You have to be able to offload work; you have to be able to delegate; you have to transition yourself from a worker to a CEO and focus on how to build value in your business.

Ask yourself the question, "How long can I stay away from the business and it still functions?" If the answer is, "I can't do it for three hours," you have a long way to go. You need to start getting to work. If you can get away for a week, two weeks without having to be involved in your business, you are well on your way, you already have a valuable business.

Congratulations! That's where you want to be.

KEY INGREDIENTS

Let's go through some of the things I have found you need to focus on to maximize the value of your business so you do become a favorable target for buyers.

REVENUE

The first thing, as I mentioned already, is *recurring revenue*. The next is *predictable revenue*.

These are a must. Recurring revenue is what buyers are going to look for. In my business, the majority of my clients were on recurring revenue. If you can get *fixed fee recurring revenue*, that's even better because it's predictable. It's easy for a buyer to predict what kind of revenue, cashflow, profit, they could wean off of your business.

Next, you've got your *recurring hourly* clients. They're fairly predictable as well. Even though they are billed hourly, it's probably going to be close to the same amount every month. Buyers are still going to like that.

The rung below that, you might have straight *hourly* work. It might be special project work that you're not really sure how many hours you're going to bill yet. Some months, it's small. Some months, it's large. Some months you don't get any and then they come back two or three months later. Buyers will consider that revenue, but how much weight they're going to put into that type of client is uncertain, unless you've had that client for a year or two, they'll factor that into the valuation.

You want *recurring revenue* and you want *predictable revenue*. Those are by far the top two things you need to focus on.

In terms of revenue, I'd love to get everybody to a million dollars. I'd love to get everybody to two million dollars. I want you to go as big as you can go, but the advice holds true even if you're at $100,000 or $300,000. This is the type of client revenue you want to try to build with your business. When you first start out, you can decide you're only going to do fixed fee recurring revenue and that's your model. When I started out, I pretty much did everything. Fixed fee at a bookkeeping level just wasn't a popular thing. It's definitely more popular now. That's now what a lot of the bookkeeping gurus are saying you should do and I agree with them, but I'm also of the mindset that I don't turn away clients just because they don't want to do that, if they'd rather do hourly.

Starting out, you absolutely should accept hourly clients; especially if you can close more business that way. As you work with your hourly clients over a length of time, you should try getting them converted over to a fixed monthly, recurring fee arrangement.

It'll make your job easier as far as billing and collection, but it will also be more valuable to your buyers.

CLIENTS

Clients are the number one value asset you've got. I'm not saying anything spectacular. They're your clients, they pay the bills, but they're ultimately what your value is based on. We always want to define what our ideal clients are but, as far as an acquisition, buyers want to see that you've got agreements in place. I didn't have an agreement for every one of my clients, but in the due diligence process, they're going to ask for them. If you have agreements in place, that certainly helps, but what helps most of all with client is *tenure*. If you can show that your clients have been doing business with you for years, the importance of an agreement or a contract isn't as much. They trust that client is going to stay with you, and most likely with the buyer through the transition. But when your buyer performs their due diligence, they are going to want to see contracts to feel safe and secure that whatever agreements you had in place with your clients are going to assign or transfer over to them without a lot of legal obstacles.

DEBT AND PROFITABILITY

Buyers also look for *low debt*. It's important you don't have a lot of debt on the books. Not all debt is bad but realize that the first chunk of money you're going to get from the sale is going to pay off your debt. So, you can't be insolvent or owe a lot of money. That could be a negative. It's not necessarily a deal-killer, but whatever you can do to clean up your balance sheet on the debt side would be worth it.

Certainly, you want to be profitable, but I don't think profitability is a deal-killer. In the bookkeeping industry, buyers want your clients. I always told people, "Just give me the revenue. I know my model can make money off of it." They're not going to come in and keep all your processes and procedures. They're not going to keep all your workflows. They're not going to keep all your vendors, insurances, and so on. They're going to come in and retool and integrate your business into their own operations.

They don't look too much at your expense structure because through their own due diligence they're going to figure out, "Well, if I drop this amount of revenue into my model, can I be profitable?" That said, if you're profitable, that gives the buyer confidence that you're running a good operation. It's *confidence* in you as a business owner and them knowing they're doing a deal with somebody who does it the right way that helps a business sell. You want to try to be profitable, with positive cashflow. In any business, you should want to be profitable, but understand a buyer really just wants your client list.

STAFF

You want to have a *good team* in place. That is, after all, how you're able to step away. You want to transition over to the CEO role as quickly as you can. When I did, I still did client work. I just focused on the higher-value jobs. I worked with maybe two or three clients on higher-end consulting and advisory work because I enjoy that work and I wanted to stay in the mix. I still wanted to know what was going on in the market—particularly the small business community. It kept me focused. It kept me engaged. It would be smart for you to build value *in you* and transition out of the low-paying stuff into the higher-paying stuff and focus on your business and the other elements we're talking about in this chapter.

You have to have a team, which means you have to hire smart; you have to fire smart, and you have to train people on your way of doing business. Build your culture, build your processes, and give clear direction on what they have to do. You have to have a good team in place. You can't step away unless you've got people that can run it. Ultimately, a buyer is going to want to move your practice over to their platform. Your team is an *asset*. Your business is certainly an asset, but your team within that business is a big part of that asset. Buyers don't just want your clients; they may want your staff as well. If you've had loyal staff who have been with you for years, have worked with your clients for years, that's huge. It's so hard in the job market to find good people so if they can pick up a staff of accountants and bookkeepers through the acquisition, that only makes your business more attractive.

I know if I was going into an acquisition, I wanted to make sure there was already a manager in place because you want to have a lot of bandwidth when you do an acquisition. If my managers are already stretched pretty thin and I bring on 200 more clients, eight more staff, is my management staff going to be able to handle that acquisition? Maybe, maybe not, but if the company I was buying already had management in place, it's just business as usual. You just change ownership. That's what you want. You want it where it's literally you're just changing the name on the ownership papers. Nothing else really in the business as far as clients, or staff changes. That's going to help your clients feel comfortable with the transition and more than likely stick around.

Focus on building a team. Even years before you decide to sell, it sure would be nice to have a vacation. I mean, I'm preaching to the choir!

EASE OF TRANSITION

Buyers want to know that when the acquisition is done, they don't have to jump through a lot of hoops to transition. It's important you have your ducks in a row. You want the due diligence phase to go smoothly.

One of the things I did right, was building different revenue streams via different divisions within my company. When I sold, I sold just one division, my most valuable division, which was the bookkeeping division. That's what I had built from scratch. That's where the majority of my staff resided. That's where the majority of my clients resided. I had all the things I've spelled out in this chapter in place, and I was able to simply sell off a segment of my business, keeping the rest of my business with my other revenue streams.

Think through how you set your company up. Do you want to set up a separate LLC for each division, like I did for my tax business? It's not always necessary to keep divisions separate, legally, in fact that seems like a lot of extra work. I have separate revenue lines on my financial statements. I had a consulting income line, I had a QuickBooks training line, and I had a bookkeeping line on my profit and loss statement. You should do that at least internally, so you can see and evaluate and build your metrics for each revenue line, and if you sell it's easy then to say to a buyer, "Everything's already categorized. Just pay attention to the bookkeeping lines since that's what I'm selling." Every buyer is going to have their own criteria, and there could be instances where it's smart to break off and set those up as separate LLCs. But, at a minimum, you should separate out revenue streams on your financial statements.

Pay attention to your balance sheet. Accounting people probably pay more attention to the balance sheet than people who aren't accountants. That's for sure. Your balance sheet is important to the value calculation of your business because that's where you list your assets. If you don't have all your assets on your balance sheet, you're short-selling yourself. Hopefully, the due diligence process uncovers any assets you don't have listed, but if the buyer has to uncover missing assets through their due diligence, it's not going to look good for you—in fact it could wreck the deal because they're not going to have confidence in any of your numbers. If you're a business that has inventory, make sure your inventory value is on your balance sheet. Bookkeeping businesses typically don't have finished goods inventory, but if you own any other type of retail business, you're more than likely going to have inventory. It's critical you show the proper amount of inventory on your balance sheet anytime you give out your financial statements.

You also want to make sure your other tangible assets (vehicles, furniture, computer equipment, etc.) are on your balance sheet. You can decide to sell those along with your clients, or not. The buyer may want all your furniture, conference room chairs, conference tables, phone systems, and servers. All that stuff needs to be accounted for on your balance sheet correctly with the right asset value. It's important you keep track of your tangible assets on your balance sheet or you might shortchange yourself in any deal you do.

Buyers want to know you have stablished a nice *sales engine* or *pipeline*. They're going to look at the last time you added a client. If the buyer is smart, they're going to look at your P&L statement or your client list and want to know when the start date was of your last six clients (random number). If you're doing this in November and your last client was signed up in March, they might be a little concerned with that. Is your business trending up, is your business flat, or is your business trending down? They're going to look at trends. You may have a decent-size book of business, but have you let your foot off the gas, or have you been continually signing up new clients? If not, that's going to raise a red flag—Maybe your reputation has recently suffered or something's going on that you're not getting new work. Is there a rumor going around about your company or have you been losing employees? What's the reason your pipeline has dried up and you haven't signed up any new clients?

Buyers want to see that you're still active, there are still leads coming in, you're still converting those leads, and that you have an active, viable, growing business.

MULTIPLE

As we discussed, your valuation really comes down to your recurring revenue. That's an easy number. It's on your profit-loss statement. Then you'll hear about what's called a *multiple*. A multiple is a subjective number buyers use to help determine the total value of your business. Typically, in the accounting industry, it's based on a factor of *one*. Accounting businesses are often valued at *one times revenue*. For example, a buyer will pay 1.2 times revenue, 1.3 times revenue or .8 of revenue. In determining your company's value, you're usually going to start at a factor of 1 or start under 1. If you're starting under 1, I don't recommend selling your business unless you're desperate. If you can't get a 1-for-1 revenue factor on the sale of your business you might want to rethink it, delay it, put it off, work on some of these things we're talking about in this chapter, and then go back to market.

The more recommendations I've outlined in this book you can checkmark and say, "I've done that," the higher your multiple is going to be. It's important you understand all these components that go into what's going to increase your multiple. I know when I was first targeted for acquisition, nobody saw any of my financials. All they saw was my *brand*. Then, a broker contacted me. Once I shared my financials with the broker, they got more serious about acquiring me because they saw the value. It's important to note I was recognized as a possible acquisition *before* anyone did any due diligence, and that's why you want to constantly build your brand, win those awards, get recognition, and put yourself out there on the map so you are noticeable to people who are out there looking for acquisition targets.

TRACKING PROGRESS

A very practical indicator of how you're doing in *building your business to be salable* is simply, as we discussed, your ability to get away and have things still run without you. The first step is to be able to get away for three hours! (Ha!) How about one month? If you can go away for a month and your business still functions, you're enjoying that lifestyle already and you don't even have to sell if you don't want to. The point of this book is to create options for yourself. You want your company to be such a huge asset that you can either stay in the business and work whenever you want with whomever you want, or you can sell. That's financial freedom. That's ultimately what you're trying to do. But you've got to put the work in. You can't just serve clients and that's it. You have to put the work in to *build your business* so you have those options for yourself.

You have to have processes and procedures in place. Your buyer will want to see that if an employee leaves, there's a how-to manual, there are instructions on how to service a client. The more structured you look and the more structured you are, the more comfortable your buyer is going to feel when you're going through your transaction. Processes and procedures are part of your infrastructure. You should make sure your infrastructure keeps up with your growth. If you're a $2 million business, your infrastructure is a lot more involved, a lot more expensive than if you're a sole proprietor doing $100,000 a year. So, continue to invest in your infrastructure.

You can't run a big business and not keep up with the technology, or the cybersecurity, appropriate to your business. It's unfortunate, but I see a lot of CPAs who are reaching retirement age and they don't have websites, they don't have portals for clients to upload documents, they don't even use email. They don't have any 21st-century technology in their business. They're still running their business the way they did when they started their firm. But now they're expecting somebody to come in and buy their book of business when the clients they're serving probably aren't going to be up to speed with the technology the buyer is going to use. A buyer is going to be nervous that the integration is not going to go well in such a case, that they're going to lose a lot of clients and the return on investment is going to be horrible. It's important you keep up your infrastructure with today's standards if you want to truly maximize the value of your business.

This is all determined as part of *due diligence*.

DUE DILIGENCE

Due diligence is the stage you enter once you and the buyer agree you're both interested in moving forward in considering a sale. Once the potential buyer submits a *letter of intent*, you formally enter a *due diligence* phase, where you open up your business to inspection, you open up your books, you open up your tax returns to the buyer and you start getting into the details. It would be great if you are planning in advance for that exit, to have all that relevant information on hand. I create folders every year with my tax returns and my personal financial statements. Then each time one of those returns is completed, I dump it in the folder. If you're a business owner and you've got any sort of debt, banks ask for those documents every year anyway, to renew lines of credit or as part of loans you might already have, you constantly have to submit your financial information. Your buyer is no different. They're going to want to see tax returns and financial statements.

LITIGATION

If you do have any litigation going on, that's going to come up in the due diligence process. It's probably going to come up even before you have a letter of intent. Nobody wants to buy into a nasty situation or potential threats of them getting weaved into litigation. You want to disclose any side agreements you might have with people or other businesses. Again, document, document. You should document everything you've got in your head at this point because, again, it looks more professional. There are no surprises, and there's a lot of confidence built up in the transaction. Of course, always try to avoid litigation, but if you do have it, make sure it gets resolved and settled before you go to sell your business.

YOUR COMPANY

In the end, it has to be about your company, and not about you as an individual, although that's how you likely will start off as you build your reputation. But in the end, when you want to sell, your real value is in your *brand*. You can't go away on vacation for any significant amount of time if you've got clients emailing and calling you, if you've got bookkeepers calling you instead of their managers. Many times, I had to push back with my bookkeepers and say, "I love you and everything, but this is not a situation you should be bringing to me, the CEO. You have a manager you should go to. If the manager can't handle the situation, that's fine, but let's cut down on the amount of interaction until it gets to the point where it's serious enough that I do need to get involved."

You'll figure out as you grow your business that the *culture* you create is the best way to remove yourself from busy work and that getting involved in every little gossipy conversation and every minute detail of office operations will suck the life out of you. You have to build your brand to the point where when a buyer or a broker is looking into your business, it's impressive. If they're searching for acquisition targets, the first thing they're going to look for is, "What's their online presence? Do they have a website? Well, yeah, they've got a website but it's not very professional. It's not very well done. They obviously didn't spend a lot of money or invest in that technology. Maybe I'll look at the next one. Maybe I'll go to your social media accounts. Are you active on social media? Are you posting inappropriate things on there?"

Internally, your brand is about your culture, about the work ethic of your people. It's about your clients. How long have they stayed with you? And your employees, how long have they stayed with you? That's just common sense. The longer your clients have been with you, the longer your staff have been with you, the better that reflects on your brand. That's what a buyer is going to look at. That's going to increase the value of your business. Nobody likes it if you're constantly dealing with turnover, whether with clients or staff. That just slows you down. You're not going to scale and you're not going to grow to a million dollars if you're constantly flipping employees and constantly flipping clients. You have to invest in best practices so people stay around. And the longer they're with you, the more value you get when you go to sell. Ultimately, you always want to run your business with this in mind.

I mentioned my mindset shifted once I read *Built to Sell*. I have always been the type of person who plans ahead. I'm always trying to be three or four steps ahead of the curve and be very proactive. *Built to Sell* inspired me to take action. And the earlier you do, the better off you're going to be. It's never too late to do a lot of these things, but the earlier you can start on them, the better. People often feel they want to know it all before they start something – maybe it's the next phase of your business' growth strategy. They feel they have to have all the answers and they have to have everything lined up and in place before they start, and that's just not how it works. You actually have to do something. Sometimes you fail, sometimes you succeed, and that will show you the path. I have changed my path so many times, and it can get frustrating for your employees, but don't feel like you have to know it all right away. Don't try to be perfect or convince yourself to wait for the "right time" because that time rarely presents itself.

Make a list all the things I've mentioned in this chapter. See if you can check them off, and start with, "How long can I be away from my business without it falling apart?" Part of that answer is your ego. A lot of business owners think the whole thing will come off the tracks if they're gone for 15 minutes. Well, you and I both know that's not true. That's your ego talking. You're going to put a lot more value on yourself and your involvement than maybe there really is.

If you can't be away from your business for three hours, you got big problems. You've got to take a good look and give yourself an honest answer to the question, "How long can I be away?" Take your ego out of the equation. Take your pride out of the equation, because your ego and your pride can be satisfied *when you cash out!* That's when you can beat your chest and tell people how great you are because you built a really solid business that you sold for a lot of money. That's your reward for being an awesome business owner.

[10] EXIT STRATEGY

EVERYTHING WE'VE DONE up to this point is to get you focused on the *value and ease of sale of your business or sale of part of it*. You need to get out of the mindset that your business is a day-to-day job and think more about your future, think about your family in the long-term. You should never take your foot off the gas when it comes to your business and planning. Even before you start your business, you should be thinking about how you're going to exit your business. If you don't have an exit strategy, you need to get one or two or three because it's guaranteed that your exit strategy is likely to change over time. I knew going into my business that I was going to succeed and there was going to be an exit strategy. I knew I wanted and needed to grow it as an *asset*.

I'm the type person who is going to work as long as I can breathe. When people say "retirement," the definition is different for different people. My definition of retirement is along the lines of financial freedom. That's what I took from Robert Kiyosaki's book, *Rich Dad, Poor Dad*. I'm at the stage in my life and my career where I want to bring in as much money as I can by doing as little work as possible. I want to be able to control my work schedule 100%. But I've earned that. On that journey, you're going to work your butt off, right? You're probably working a lot more than what you're getting paid for, in fact.

Your *exit strategy* is when you flip that around. You're overworked and underpaid for many years of business ownership. It's going to hurt your pride at times. You're going to feel like it's not worth it at times, but you have to keep your eye on the prize and know that the tables will turn and it will get to a point where you're working far fewer hours for either the same amount of money or hopefully much more money. That's what you need to focus on.

FAMILY TIES

My initial thought was this would be an ongoing business for me. Either somebody within my company would take it over and I would go off into the sunset as some kind of chairman who just comes in for board meetings, or see my company eventually run by my kids. If you can find somebody in-house and reward them for years of service by having them take over, it's a great reward and a great opportunity for your staff. The problem is that not everybody's qualified to run a business, and even if they are, many don't want the stress and it might not be for them. In my case, there wasn't anybody in-house who wanted to step up and take that path or I would have handed the keys over to them. I thought, *Maybe one of my children will come up in the business.* While they both got exposure to accounting classes in college, neither of them was interested or suited to work in the business. I had to pivot. As soon as I knew it wasn't going to be a family business and there wasn't going to be an existing employee taking over, the only option at that point was to sell. I actually didn't put my business up for sale, I was approached by a business broker.

And this is where we come back to being open to *opportunities*.

If people reach out to you, whether it's on LinkedIn, social media, email, phone calls, whatever it is, don't be so quick to delete the email, don't be so quick to reject the invitation. Many people shut that down immediately. I turn down way more connection requests than I accept, particularly now at this stage of my career, but you do develop a *sixth sense*, you kind of feel who might be worth talking to. If an M&A broker reaches out to me and says, "Hey, I want to talk to you about the current state of the industry, we want to talk to you about accounting firm valuations and the data that I'm seeing," I listen!

If you're ultimately going to exit your business at some point, educate yourself on the process. Hopefully this book is giving you an education on the subject, but there's a whole lot more educating you can do to prepare yourself to handle a buy-sell opportunity. Whether you're buying somebody else or somebody is buying you, you don't want to go into that without some sort of experience or somebody helping you through that process, so do as much self-education as you can.

When the broker reached out to me and said, "Hey, I'd like to talk to you about M&A activity and accounting firms," well, that rang true for me. We had just determined my son was not going to come into the business, so what better time to talk about business valuations for accounting firms? I accepted the connection request, we started talking, and eventually we got into what my exit strategy was. I went through my whole story with him, and the rest is history.

TIMING

The *timing* of when to sell can make you wonder, *Is this too soon? When's the right time?* I was 51 years old when I sold a large piece of my business. I was thinking I'd be more like 60 before I made a move like that. I figured I'd still have several more years to build the business and make it even more marketable before I felt like I was in a position to pull the trigger. But this opportunity popped up and I didn't shut it down. I didn't think, *This isn't the right time. This isn't when I planned to sell.* When I spoke with this broker, we first just talked about the accounting industry and the current M&A environment; then the conversation shifted to focus on me and whether I'd be interested in an opportunity to sell my company. Ultimately, I decided to sell the bookkeeping portion of my business because the terms were right. I knew I would retain my brand, the *Steiner Business Solutions* name, with all the brand equity I had built up over the years. I knew I didn't have to start over. I still had my business advisory clients and fractional CFO clients I could continue to work with. I still did tax, and I still did my peer group.

When they approached me, I thought to myself, *Well, 51 is young. It's certainly way ahead of my initial exit strategy.* I looked at the deal from all angles and thought, *Well, this is actually a great opportunity to make this move. It frees me up to focus more on my advisory services, more on my other business lines.* And this would free me up, giving me new challenges, which was what I wanted out of life. When I put it all together, it was the right time.

Everything we've talked about in this book starts on *day one.* Don't wait to be open to opportunities until a certain age. Actually, if you pay attention, it starts before you even open your business. You need to constantly evaluate what your needs are. Your personal life is going to change, the industry you're in is going to change, technology is going to change, the workforce is going to change, and, if you're not paying attention to all that, you're going to end up behind the curve, you're going to miss out on the right option at the right time if you're not looking. For me, it was the right opportunity at the right time, even though it was happening perhaps *nine years* sooner than expected!

EXIT STRATEGIES

MERGERS

As for exit strategies, there are several to be open to and to look for. Probably best-known are *mergers* and *acquisitions*, referred to as "M&A." A *merger* is a valid exit strategy, and a merger can be part of your growth strategy. If you find another business in your industry, perhaps another bookkeeping firm, you might one day *merge* your operations with their operations. If you do, you'll have to make several decisions:

- Whose name do we keep?
- Are we going to keep all the staff?
- Are we going to keep all the office locations?

A merger allows you to bring on a partner who can take some of the burden off of you, whether it's a financial burden or a management burden. If you just don't want all that stress on you anymore, or you don't feel you're capable of taking your business to the next level, and you've found somebody who might be a little further ahead of you in terms of their size, you might consider a merger. If you're more capable at a bookkeeping level but you want to start doing taxes or start doing CFO work, you could merge with somebody, or form a partnership with another person, combining into one company.

You might merge your businesses and still step out. You might merge your business with another company and decide you're going to retire. Or, they might pay you a monthly stipend, distribution, dividend, or salary, perhaps even with you there in a limited role. Maybe you're no longer in a CEO role but you remain as a mentor or in an advisor role. That's another way you could potentially pull value out of that merger, that whomever you merge with is going to pay you to integrate the two companies and then you can work out what your compensation plan would look like, and what your exit out of that newly combined company would look like.

ACQUISITIONS

The other part of "M&A," of course, is *acquisitions*. A full-out acquisition is where you simply sell all your assets. That's called an *asset sale* The buyer is only buying your assets, not your corporate entity. After the sale, you are basically stepping away; although you might be involved in helping with the transition. The point is that you might exit via a full acquisition, or through a partial acquisition like I did, selling only part of your company. In recent years, there has been a lot of M&A activity in the accounting industry. There are a lot of older CPAs leaving the market, and a new generation of young professionals coming in with a lot of technological expertise who are seeing opportunities to scale their businesses quickly. You've got to be aware of that. You have to know who the buyers are out there, what multiples they're paying, and what they're looking for. Often, such acquisitions are published and you can easily find out about them.

At the same time, you don't really hear about many bookkeeping acquisitions. I don't think there are that many. Honestly, that's in part why I'm writing this book, because it seems too many bookkeepers are building their businesses only to let them go without getting full (or any) value for them. I'm here to say there's opportunity there! If you want to grow, you should be reaching out to these bookkeeping people on social media and asking them if they are looking to sell and if they have an exit strategy. It's nice if you can contact them and lay out some options because you read my book. You should be educated enough now, as part of your growth strategy, to start putting out offers, knowing how to structure those offers and what to look for, because those opportunities are out there if you're willing to reach out.

There are a lot of buyers out there as well, and a lot of these buyers may not be your traditional bookkeeping people. There is a lot of *tech* getting into this space. There are software companies buying up bookkeeping companies. These buyers want access to small business owners, and you as bookkeepers have that access. So, the bigger your book of business (I had access to around 300 small businesses), the more attractive you are to buyers. The buyers out there are not simply just other bookkeeping companies or bookkeepers. They're big companies with an appetite who want access to your clients, not only to provide bookkeeping services to them but to provide other services to them as well. When I talked to this broker about my deal, he laid out all the players who are out there in the market for acquisition. Some of them didn't surprise me, but there were definitely several I would never have guessed had an appetite for acquiring bookkeeping companies.

So, don't limit your thinking. If you have the ability to grow and scale, there is a market for your business and there's a market for your clients. As I was growing my company, I was a little worried I was going to get too big. That kind of thinking goes against everything I'm talking about in this book, I know, but I really was concerned. I thought there was such a small market with few buyers out there who could digest a $2 million company. Even before I got to a million dollars, I was always thinking, *Gosh, is this going to shrink my buyer pool?* When you're doing $100,000 a year or $200,000 a year, there's no question your buyer pool should be greater. There are a lot more people out there who can afford and integrate a $200,000 business than a $2 million business.

The bigger I got, the more I paid attention to the market. It was a legitimate concern of mine that I was going to get too big. And I only thought about my local market, so I thought, *Who in Richmond, Virginia, can buy my entire company for $2 million?* I went through my list of competitors and other accounting firms and that was a small, small list. That concerned me, but after talking to this broker I met on LinkedIn, I saw that the buyers out there are some of the big boys, and I suddenly felt *smaller!*

I know now there are a ton of opportunities out there, so I am not concerned anymore that you can be too big. In fact, you can't be. There is absolutely a market of buyers out there who will buy your firm. And the point of this book is to make sure you get as much money out of that deal as possible. I've done it. I have been exposed to the current market and the appetite that is out there. I was thinking too small! I didn't devalue what I thought my business was worth, I devalued the pool of potential buyers. I just didn't think there were many bookkeeping companies out there that could handle me. This new knowledge dispels that myth. There *is* a market, but you have got to know it and you have got to pay attention to it. You have got to talk to people and you have got to put in the work. You always have to be focusing on planning your eventual exit.

POST-EXIT

I'm 51, and I was not prepared to go off into the sunset. I had a lot of years ahead of me and I had to provide for my family. This wasn't going to be the end for me. Selling my business was a great strategic move and I knew I had a plan for going forward. I knew what my plan was, *post exit*. As much as you need to plan your exit—and "planning" is basically the entire lifecycle of your business up to the point you close the deal—you should be planning your post-exit strategy. And it would be the same advice I gave before—You follow the same thought processes, same ideas of revenue streams, same practice of documenting everything and building a *valuable* business.

I'm already thinking about my *next* exit strategy! I'm rebuilding and retooling Steiner Business Solutions for the next 5-10 years and it's exciting because it's a new challenge for me. I don't know what is ahead for me, but I have the financial freedom to continue to take risks and call the shots.

I am still early into my post-exit life. I knew going in I wanted to continue to do consulting and advisory services, but I'm looking at other opportunities as well. This book is one of my post-exit strategies, actually. I asked myself, *How can I leverage my success? How can I help other people do the same thing?* That's an exciting adventure for me!

What is my next exit? What does it look like to get to 60 years old? I've got a successful tax business. I've got high-value clients I currently work with. My goal now is to recreate more revenue streams, but I'm going to recreate these revenue streams working a lot fewer hours. That's what I want. That's where it's exciting for me in my post-exit life, is that I can now decide how many hours I want to work. It may just be 10 or 20 hours a week. Maybe I only want to work virtually. Maybe I only want to work with a handful of clients. Either direction, I have the freedom to pick my path and I'm having a great time figuring out what challenges I want to tackle on my new professional journey.

So, work on that post-exit strategy as well. Think about what's next for you. Have you thought about life after your exit? I mean, that's an exciting time. You've got to put in the work, you've got to follow my advice throughout this book, and if you do, you will absolutely reap the rewards. As Zig Ziglar says, "Strategy is nothing without execution."

To help, I offer coaching and mentoring services to business-owner clients supporting them as they implement and execute all the advice I laid out in this book. Please see the back of the book to sign up for my free initial consulting offer.

You can do this! Don't think small. Think big. Be willing to pivot from one thing to the next. Don't miss out on opportunities. The best advice I could give is to *pay attention.* Pay attention to everything. Don't get tunnel vision where you get sucked into the day-to-day operations alone. It's very hard not to do that, but you have a business, a brand, and value to build. Get competitive and pay attention. Opportunities are everywhere! You have to identify them and you have to *act on them.* Reaching the pinnacle of your own liquidity event comes from identifying opportunities and taking risks. It's developing your network of business contacts. It's studying your industry, studying your competition. You are a CEO. You cannot just be a bookkeeper. You cannot just be a doer. You're going to make mistakes, but you have to be the CEO.

THINK BIGGER

If you don't think this is possible for you, *think bigger.* I did, and you can too.

Appendix A:
Indispensable
Marketing

by Patrick McFadden
Marketing Consultant to Steiner Business Solutions

I'VE WORKED WITH Dan Steiner and Steiner Business Solutions for years, and we've enjoyed great success, as his book *Think Bigger* details. Dan asked me to explain the success of our SEO program and how this has impacted Steiner Business Solutions, and I'm happy to do so.

One of the key things we did for Steiner Business Solutions when we were getting started was understanding not only the vision and the mission Dan had for his business, but who his ideal customers were, determining what keywords and phrases these types of customers type into Google to look for a solution or a vendor or business like Steiner Business Solutions.

That insight of understanding who Dan's ideal clients were helped craft the keywords we should be going after. Quite frankly, in the industry of accounting and bookkeeping, everyone is so far behind in terms of SEO that Steiner Business Solutions has been in spot one in search results for months or even years. They've been able to dominate the market, even to the point now that when I type in "small business bookkeeping Richmond," not only does Dan's Google My Business profile pop up, if you scroll past the ad his business appears several levels above even Yelp, which is hard to beat as it's an *aggregator* or a *directory*.

It's hard to beat these because they have a much greater amount of traffic, even a greater number of keywords. In fact, my research tool here says Steiner Business Solutions has eight keywords, whereas Yelp has 1.01 *million* keywords! It's insane, but we've done a good job at getting Steiner to be on the first page of Google, even to the point where if you were to scroll further down, the search results include Dan's related businesses. You find Steiner Tax Services there. So it's been amazing.

With SEO, the process is all the same, whether for an accountant, a lawyer, a book or product, or a website. The only difference is knowing your strategy, which is based upon the type of customers that you want to attract. For example, high-end customers might not type "cheap services Richmond," they might type "the best services." So, it all starts with strategy which again, is based around who your customer is and what problems you solve for that type of customer. That is then infused into your SEO strategy because you want to attract the type of customers that you're well suited to serve.

For us, in determining the strategy part of the marketing and discovering who we are going to reach out to, it's part conversation with the owner, part conversation with the staff, and conversations with actual clients. We ask them very pointed questions, such as:

- "How would you look for a service like this?

- What things do you research when you're selecting a bookkeeper or an accounting firm?

- Where do you spend your time?

- What phrases would you type into Google to look for a provider like this?"

With that type of research and interviews, we're able to craft a persona that's based off their best customers and find where they hang out, how they would type their phrases into Google, and what elements of the website would appeal to this type of customer. They may not look at reviews. They may care about your best nominated credentialed awards or seeing a video of a past customer like them resonate more to them than just saying you have five-star reviews. So, we use that kind of strategy to dictate the marketing. It's almost like medicine. You do a diagnosis of what is and that determines the prescription you write. Well, we do a diagnosis of the customer to determine what marketing you should do.

There are certain tactical aspects. For example, you have to have a certain amount of content on a page for it to rank so you want to sprinkle your keywords and phrases throughout the content and even in the page title. If you have the information that people are looking for, and if more people are finding you and Google acknowledges that, you tend to dominate for that keyword or phrase.

With the accounting industry today, frankly, the marketing is weak. I mean, typically, to be ranked number one or even be on page one of Google, it usually takes about three to six months and it varies based on the competition. But because most accountants and bookkeeping firms are not savvy at SEO, Dan was able to get on page one within, I believe, 30 to 60 days. That's in part a testament to how bad the industry is by not believing clients come from the internet and not actively maintaining their SEO.

It's just like your lawn at home. You have to mow your grass every week or every month. Companies will often hire an SEO company to come in and do the foundational work one time and then say, "Well, it's done. Let's sit back and let it rain." But SEO is like a sport. Everybody else is beefing up their muscles while you're sitting back, so if you don't have a way to continually work out your SEO muscles, you're going to get triumphed over. That's what happens in the accounting and certain other industries, but Dan made an investment, and it is an investment. He is still an ongoing monthly client where he pays us to maintain not only his SEO but all his marketing, which in Dan's case includes his SEO for his website and maintaining his Google My Business profile.

Google My Business profiles enable you to be found on Google Maps and on the Google search engine. These profiles are often ignored, but for a lot of businesses you actually get more phone calls from your Google My Business profile than you do from your website. In fact, you could probably eliminate your website if you were to optimize your Google My Business profile effectively. Like everything, you could build it, but you also need to get it found, just as you need to optimize your website so it gets found.

Patrick McFadden | @patmmarketing
Founder & Marketing Consultant
p: 804.921.7159 | skype: indispensablemarketing
e: pmcfadden@indispensablemarketing.com
w: indispensablemarketing.com
Install Marketing as a Process

About the Author

Dan Steiner
Chief Executive Officer

THE FOUNDER AND OWNER of Steiner Business Solutions since its formation in 2006, Dan Steiner has accumulated 30 years of experience in financial and operational management, which he's used to help hundreds of businesses improve their performance and find their way to success.

Dan holds a BBA in Accounting from James Madison University and began his career as an auditor with Price Waterhouse, an international public accounting firm. This position enabled him to work with a variety of clients in a number of industries. Over the years, his skills and ambition led Dan to hold other high-level financial positions such as Chief Financial Officer in various companies. His experience has been working closely with business owners, providing them information and strategic guidance to help set the direction for their businesses.

Steiner Business Solutions was one of the first companies in Richmond, Virginia to offer outsourced accounting and CFO services to the market. Through Dan's leadership, SBS has built a great reputation in the business community and received several local awards in recognition of its achievements.

https://www.steinerbusinesssolutions.com

LEARN MORE

Lucky people GET opportunities;

Brave people CREATE opportunities;

And Winners CONVERT problems into opportunities.

For information about Steiner Business Solutions, coaching and mentoring services, author interviews, appearances, and speaking engagements, please contact:

Steiner Business Solutions

Corporate Office

2727 Enterprise Parkway

Suite 105

Henrico, VA 23294

(866) 314-6632

www.steinerbusinesssolutions.com

PLEASE LEAVE A REVIEW

What Did You Think of *Think Bigger*?

Thank you for purchasing *Think Bigger*. You could have picked any book, but you picked mine, and for that I'm grateful. I hope it added value and quality to your life. If so, it would be really nice if you could share this book with your friends and family:

- You can post your thoughts to Facebook and Twitter.
- I'd like to hear from you and hope that you could take some time to post a review on Amazon. Your feedback and support will help me greatly to make this book even better.

Thanks for reading!

—Dan